EVERYDAY FORMS OF PEASANT RESISTANCE IN SOUTH-EAST ASIA

EVERYDAY FORMS
OF PEASANT RESISTANCE
IN SOUTH-EAST ASIA

Edited by
JAMES C. SCOTT
and
BENEDICT J. TRIA KERKVLIET

LONDON AND NEW YORK

First published 1986 in Great Britain by
Routledge
2 Park Square, Milton Park, Abingdon, Oxon, OX14 4RN
270 Madison Ave, New York NY 10016

Transferred to Digital Printing 2006

British Library Cataloguing in Publication Data

Everyday forms of peasant resistance in
South-East Asia.—(The Journal of
peasant studies, ISSN 0306-6150; v.13,
no. 2)
1. Peasant uprisings—Asia South-
eastern   2. Peasantry—Asia, South-
eastern—Political activity
I. Scott, James C.   II. Kerkvliet,
Benedict J. Tria   III. Series
322.4'4'0959   HD880.8.263

ISBN 0-7146-3296-1

This group of studies first appeared in a Special Issue on
Everyday Forms of Peasant Resistance in South-east
Asia of *The Journal of Peasant Studies*, Vol. 13, Nos. 2,
published by Routledge

Publisher's Note
The publisher has gone to great lengths to ensure the quality of this reprint
but points out that some imperfections in the original may be apparent

Contents

Introduction   1

Everyday Forms of Peasant Resistance   James C. Scott   5

Patrolling the Middle-Ground:
  Methodological Perspectives on
  'Everyday Peasant Resistance'   Andrew Turton   36

Everyday Resistance, Socialist
  Revolution and Rural Development:
  The Vietnamese Case   Christine Pelzer White   49

From Footdragging to Flight: The Evasive
  History of Peasant Avoidance Protest
  in South and South-east Asia   Michael Adas   64

Tenants' Non-Violent Resistance to
  Landowner Claims in a Central Luzon
  Village   Brian Fegan   87

Everyday Resistance to Injustice in a
  Philippine Village   Benedict J. Tria Kerkvliet 107

Plantation Politics and Protest on
  Sumatra's Coast   Ann Laura Stoler   124

Seminar: Everyday Forms of Peasant
  Resistance (A Poem)   Ina Slamet
                                              (tr. by Ben White)   144

Introduction

Studies of the peasantry over the past two decades have gone a long way towards accomplishing for this class roughly what George Rudé and others have done for 'the crowd'. Gone is the dominant image of peasants as either supine victims of historical forces or, at the polar extreme, enraged, inchoate rebels in the grip of a millennial vision. The more simplistic views of why peasants rebel and how they rebel have been replaced by far more fine-grained, complex interpretations based on careful research. These interpretations have in turn, provoked debate and inspired new theories.

The contributions to this issue of *The Journal of Peasant Studies* are not, however, concerned with the comparatively rare occasions on which peasants – alone or in league with others – openly and violently confront the state and/or agrarian elites. Instead, the authors focus on a vast and relatively unexplored middle-ground of peasant politics between passivity and open, collective defiance. The general rubric for these phenomena is 'everyday resistance' – a term that is self-consciously homely. Under this concept may plausibly be grouped the ordinary weapons of many subordinate groups – ranging all the way from clandestine arson and sabotage, to footdragging, dissimulation, false-compliance, pilfering, slander, flight, and so forth. Although varied, such forms of resistance have certain features in common. They require little or no co-ordination or planning; they often represent forms of 'self-help'; they typically avoid any direct symbolic affront to authority; and they are generally underwritten by a sub-culture of resistance. The initial premise is that such forms of resistance, though less dramatic or headline-worthy than uprisings, are more or less constant and constitute the normal means by which the peasantry resists claims on its surplus. A further premise is that 'routine' resistance of this kind may, cumulatively, have an appreciable impact on class and authority relations in the countryside.

This premise was the idea behind a December 1982 conference of Southeast Asian specialists held at the Institute of Social Studies in The Hague and supported by the Social Science Research Council (New York). With the lively conference discussions in mind, several participants agreed to revise their papers for *The Journal of Peasant Studies*.

Little more can be said about what contributors say collectively about the characteristics of everyday resistance because, as the reader will see, there are several points of disagreement. Before highlighting the prominent unresolved issues, let us note areas of consensus.

All writers agree that scholars should pay attention to the less obvious and non-confrontational forms of resistance and protest. (Christine White and Andrew Turton caution, though, against focusing on such resistance to the exclusion of other aspects of peasant society, particularly power relationships within peasant households, among peasants, and between peasants and others.) They also agree that not everything the peasantry does to survive constitutes resistance. Survival strategies which, for example, involve predatory behaviour between peasants, would not count. To constitute resistance, the act must be at the expense of or be directed toward super-ordinates, not equals or subordinates. Third, those wrestling with the problem of how to identify everyday resistance concur that intention is important.

The authors here, however, are not in accord about what is required in order to ascertain intention nor how exactly to differentiate everyday resistance from various survival methods. Assessing intention is difficult, especially if one is relying heavily, as Michael Adas does, on historical documents. But there are problems even if the researcher has, as several of the contributors do, information from interviews and observation.

Although Christine White never says explicitly what constitutes resistance, we infer from what she says it is *not*, and from her examples, that her criteria are more limiting than those of others. She seems to distinguish ''resistance'' in quotes, from real resistance, at least in a colonial or capitalistic system. Real resistance decisively alters colonial or capitalistic state policies or contributes to transforming the system, not just delaying the advance of exploitative policies of, say, the state and landlords. Similarly, ''resistance'' is only a safety valve and contributes to a false-consciousness, giving peasants temporary relief and thus obscuring the extent of their power-lessness and exploitation.

At the other end of our spectrum is James Scott's argument. He objects to those who insist that resistance must contribute to revolutionary consequences and/or be selfless. Resistance can even have unintended con-sequences. The subject of Ann Stoler's article is an example. Stoler shows that although peasants protested against plantation policies in Sumatra and often fled in order to establish autonomous villages and means of sub-sistence, the results were more in the interests of capital than not. For Scott, resistance is whatever peasants do to deny to mitigate claims by appropriat-ing classes or to press their own claims *vis-à-vis* these superordinate classes. This includes a far wider range of activities than White would permit.

Other contributors take intermediate positions. Brian Fegan contends that resistance requires not only that peasants intend to withhold grain or other resources from, say, a landlord but that fellow peasants concur that it is right to evade the appropriating class member's claims. Benedict Kerkvliet also emphasises the importance of the peasants' conception of justice in their acts of resistance but does not require the consensus that Fegan does Adas has revised his earlier position, which held that avoidance protest must have harmful consequences known by both the peasant and his adversary-target. His position is now closer to that of Scott than that of White.

Although all the authors here are specialists on South-east Asia, the phenomena that comprise everyday resistance are hardly limited to that region. Indeed, several authors draw widely upon literature outside the region. Our hope is that these articles will encourage scholars to pursue the subject and the debates surrounding it in other agrarian settings. At a minimum, we hope these debates will promote a view of peasant politics that embraces a far wider terrain than has been customarily ploughed. An account of peasant protest devoted exclusively to uprisings and collective protests would be no more justifiable than an account of factory workers' protest devoted entirely to major strikes and riots.

JIM SCOTT
BEN KERKVLIET

Everyday Forms of Peasant Resistance

Jim Scott*

I. THE UNWRITTEN HISTORY OF RESISTANCE

The argument which follows originated in a growing dissatisfaction with much of the recent work – my own as well as that of others – on the subject of peasant rebellion and revolution. It is only too apparent that the inordinate attention to large-scale peasant insurrection was, in North America at least, stimulated by the Vietnam war and something of a left-wing academic romance with wars of national liberation. In this case interest and source material were mutually reinforcing. For the historical and archival records were richest at precisely those moments when the peasantry came to pose a threat to the state and to the existing international order.[1] At other times, which is to say most of the time, the peasantry appeared in the historical record not so much as historical actors but as more or less anonymous contributors to statistics on conscription, taxes, labour migration, land holdings, and crops production.

The fact is that, for all their importance when they do occur, peasant rebellions, let alone peasant 'revolutions', are few and far between. Not only are the circumstances which favour large-scale peasant uprising comparatively rare, but when they do appear, the revolts which develop are nearly always crushed unceremoniously. To be sure, even a failed revolt may achieve something: a few concessions from the state or landlords, a brief respite from new and painful relations of production[2] and, not least, a memory of resistance and courage that may lie in wait for the future. Such gains, however, are uncertain, while the carnage, the repression, and the demoralization of defeat are all too certain and real.

In a larger sense one might say that the historiography of class struggle has been systematically distorted in a state-centric direction. The events that claim attention are the events to which the state and ruling classes accord most attention in their archives. Thus, for example, a small and futile rebellion claims an attention all out of proportion to its impact on class relations while unheralded acts of flight, sabotage, theft which may have far greater impact are rarely noticed. The small rebellion may have a symbolic importance for its violence and for its revolutionary aims but for most subordinate classes historically such rare episodes were of less moment than the quiet, unremitting guerrilla warfare that took place day-in and day-out. It is perhaps only in the study of slavery that such forms of resistance are

*Department of Political Science, Yale University, P.O. Box 3532 Yale Station, New Haven, CT 06520–3532, USA.

given due attention, and that is clearly because there have been relatively few slave rebellions (in the antebellum South at any rate) to whet the historian's appetite. It is also worth recalling as well that even at those extraordinary historical moments when a peasant-backed revolution actually succeeds in taking power, the results are, at the very best, a mixed blessing for the peasantry. Whatever else the revolution may achieve, it almost always creates a more coercive and hegemonic state apparatus – one that is often able to batten itself on the rural population like no other before it. All too frequently the peasantry finds itself in the ironic position of having helped to power a ruling group whose plans for industrialisation, taxation, and collectivisation are very much at odds with the goals for which peasants had imagined they were fighting.[3]

A history of the peasantry which only focused on uprisings would be much like a history of factory workers devoted entirely to major strikes and riots. Important and diagnostic though these exceptional events may be, they tell us little about the most durable arena of class conflict and resistance: the vital, day-to-day struggle on the factory floor over the pace of work, over leisure, wages, autonomy, privileges, and respect. For workers operating, by definition, at a structural disadvantage and subject to repression, such forms of quotidian struggle may be the only option available. Resistance of this kind does not throw up the manifestos, demonstrations, and pitched battles that normally compel attention, but vital territory is being won and lost here too. For the peasantry, scattered across the countryside and facing even more imposing obstacles to organised, collective action, everyday forms of resistance would seem particularly important.

For all these reasons it occurred to me that the emphasis on peasant rebellion was misplaced. Instead, it seemed far more germane to understand what we might call *everyday* forms of peasant resistance – the prosaic but constant struggle between the peasantry and those who seek to extract labour, food, taxes, rents, and interest from them. Most of the forms this struggle takes stop well short of collective outright defiance. Here I have in mind the *ordinary* weapons of relatively powerless groups: footdragging, dissimulation, false-compliance, pilfering, feigned ignorance, slander, arson, sabotage, and so forth. These Brechtian forms of class struggle have certain features in common. They require little or no co-ordination or planning; they often represent a form of individual self-help; and they typically avoid any direct symbolic confrontation with authority or with elite norms. To understand these commonplace forms of resistance is to understand what much of the peasantry does 'between revolts' to defend its interests as best it can.

It would be a grave mistake, as it is with peasant rebellions, overly to romanticise these 'weapons of the weak'. They are unlikely to do more than marginally affect the various forms of exploitation which peasants confront. Furthermore, the peasantry has no monopoly on these weapons, as anyone who has observed officials and landlords resisting and disrupting state policies which are to their disadvantage can easily attest.

On the other hand, such Brechtian (or Schweikian) modes of resistance are not trivial. Desertion and evasion of conscription and of corvée labour have undoubtedly limited the imperial aspirations of many a monarch in South-east Asia[4] or, for that matter, in Europe. The process, and its potential impact is nowhere better captured than in R.C. Cobb's account of draft resistance and desertion in post-revolutionary France and under the early Empire.

> From the year V to the year VII, there are increasingly frequent reports, from a variety of Departments ... of every conscript from a given canton having returned home and living there unmolested. Better still, many of them did not return home; they had never left it in the first place .... In the year VII too the severed fingers of right hands – the commonest form of self-mutilation – begin to witness statistically to the strength of what might be described as a vast movement of collective complicity, involving the family, the parish, the local authorities, whole cantons.

Even the Empire, with a vastly more numerous and reliable rural police, did not succeed in more than

> temporarily slowing down the speed of the hemorrhage which ... from 1812, once more reached catastrophic proportions. There could have been no more eloquent referendum on the universal unpopularity of an oppressive regime; and there is no more encouraging spectacle for a historian than a people that has decided it will no longer fight and that, without fuss, returns home ... the common people, at least in this respect, had their fair share in bringing down France's most appalling regime.[5]

In a similar fashion, flight and evasion of taxes have classically curbed the ambition and reach of Third World states – whether pre-colonial, colonial, or independent. Small wonder that such a large share of the tax receipts of Third World states is collected in the form of levies on imports and exports; the pattern is, in no small measure, a tribute to the tax resistance capacities of their subjects. Even a casual reading of the literature on rural 'development' yields a rich harvest of unpopular government schemes and programmes which have been nibbled to extinction by the passive resistance of the peasantry.[6] On some occasions this resistance has become active, even violent. More often, however, it takes the form of passive non-compliance, subtle sabotage, evasion and deception. The persistent efforts of the colonial government in Malaya to discourage the peasantry from growing rubber which would compete with the plantation sector for land and markets is a case in point.[7] Various restrictions schemes and land use laws were tried from 1922 until 1928 and again in the 1930s with only modest results because of massive peasant resistance. The efforts of peasants in self-styled socialist states to prevent and then to mitigate, or even undo, unpopular forms of collective agriculture represent a striking example of the defensive techniques available to a beleagured peasantry. Again the struggle is marked less by massive and defiant confrontations than by a quiet evasion that is equally massive and often far more effective.

The style of resistance in question is perhaps best described by contrasting paired forms of resistance, each aimed at much the same goal, the first of which is 'everyday' resistance in our meaning and the second the more open, direct confrontations that typically dominate the study of resistance. In one sphere lies the quiet, piecemeal process by which peasant 'squatters' have often encroached on plantation and state forest lands; in the other a public invasion of property that openly challenges property relations. In one sphere lies a process of gradual military desertion; in the other an open mutiny aiming at eliminating or replacing officers. In one sphere lies the pilfering of public or private grain stores; in the other an open attack on markets or granaries aiming at the redistribution of the food supply.

Such techniques of resistance are well adapted to the particular characteristics of the peasantry. Being a diverse class of 'low classness', geographically distributed, often lacking the discipline and leadership that would encourage opposition of a more organised sort, the peasantry is best suited to extended guerrilla-style campaigns of attrition which require little or no co-ordination. Their individual acts of footdragging and evasion, reinforced often by a venerable popular culture of resistance, and multiplied many-thousand fold may, in the end, make an utter shambles of the policies dreamed up by their would-be superiors in the capital. The state may respond in a variety of ways. Policies may be recast in line with more realistic expectations. They may be retained but reinforced with positive incentives aimed at encouraging voluntary compliance. And, of course, the state may simply choose to employ more coercion. Whatever the response, we must not miss the fact that the action of the peasantry has thus changed or narrowed the policy options available. It is in this fashion, and not through revolts, let alone legal political pressure, that the peasantry has classically made its political presence felt. Thus any history or theory of peasant politics which attempts to do justice to the peasantry as an historical actor must necessarily come to grips with what I have chosen to call 'everyday forms of resistance'. For this reason alone it is important both to document and to bring some conceptual order to this seeming welter of human activity.

Everyday forms of resistance make no headlines. Just as millions of anthozoan polyps create, willy-nilly, a coral reef, so do thousands upon thousands of individual acts of insubordination and evasion create a political or economic barrier reef of their own. There is rarely any dramatic confrontation, any moment that is particularly newsworthy. And whenever, to pursue the simile, the ship of state runs aground on such a reef, attention is typically directed to the shipwreck itself and not to the vast aggregation of petty acts which made it possible. It is very rare that the perpetrators of these petty acts seek to call attention to themselves. Their safety lies in their anonymity. It is *also* extremely rare that officials of the state wish to publicise the insubordination.[8] To do so would be to admit that their policy is unpopular and, above all, to expose the tenuousness of their authority in the countryside – neither of which the sovereign state finds in its interest.[9] The nature of the acts themselves and the self-interested muteness of the antagonists thus conspire to create a kind of complicitous silence which all but expunges everyday forms of resistance from the historical record.

History and social science, written by an intelligentsia using written records which are also created largely by literate officials, is simply not well equipped to uncover the silent and anonymous forms of class struggle which typify the peasantry.[10] In this case, its practitioners implicitly join the conspiracy of the participants who are themselves, as it were, sworn to secrecy. Collectively, this unlikely cabal contributes to a stereotype of the peasantry, enshrined in both literature and in history, as a class which alternates between long periods of abject passivity and brief, violent, and futile explosions of rage.

> He had centuries of fear and submission behind him, his shoulders had become hardened to blows, his soul so crushed that he did not recognise his own degradation. You could beat him and starve him and rob him of everything, year in, year out, before he would abandon his caution and stupidity, his mind filled with all sorts of muddled ideas which he could not properly understand; and this went on until a culmination of injustice and suffering flung him at his master's throat like some infuriated domestic animal who had been subjected to too many thrashings [*Zola*, 1980: 91].

There is a grain of truth in Zola's view, but only a grain. It is true that the 'on-stage' behaviour of peasants during times of quiescence yields a picture of submission, fear, and caution. By contrast, peasant insurrections seem like visceral reactions of blind fury. What is missing from the account of 'normal' passivity is the slow, grinding, quiet struggle over rents, crops, labour, and taxes in which submission and stupidity is often no more than a pose – a necessary tactic. What is missing from the picture of the periodic 'explosions' is the underlying vision of justice which informs them and their specific goals and targets which are often quite rational indeed. The 'explosions' themselves are frequently a sign that the 'normal' and largely covert forms of class struggle are failing or have reached a crisis point. Such declarations of open war, with their mortal risks, normally come only after a protracted struggle on different terrain.

II. TWO DIAGNOSITC EXAMPLES

In the interest of pursuing the analytical issues raised by everyday forms of resistance, I offer a brief description of two examples, among many encountered in the course of field research in a Malaysian rice-farming village from 1978 to 1980. One involved an attempt by women transplanting groups to boycott landowners who had first hired combine-harvesters to replace hand labour. The second was a pattern of anonymous thefts of harvested paddy which appeared to be increasing in frequency. Each of these two activities had the characteristic features of everyday resistance. Neither the boycott, as we shall see, nor the thefts presented any *public* or symbolic challenge to the legitimacy of the production and property arrangements being resisted. Neither required any formal organisation and, in the case of the thefts of paddy, most of the activity was carried on individually at night. Perhaps the most important characteristic of these and many other such activities in the village is that, strictly speaking, they had no authors who would publicly take responsibility for them.

Background

Before examining the two proposed examples of resistance more closely, a brief sketch of the village in question and its recent economic history should help to situate this account. The village, which we shall call Sedaka, is a community of some 74 households (352 people) located on the Muda Plain in the state of Kedah, Malaysia. The Muda region has been, since the fourteenth century, the main rice-producing area on the peninsula and rice production is by far the dominant economic activity. Village stratification in Sedaka can be read, for all practical purposes, directly from the data on paddy-land ownership and farm size. The land-poor half of the village in 1979 owned only three per cent of the paddy-land farmed by villagers and farmed (including land rented in) 18 per cent of the cultivated acreage. Average farm size for this poorest half of the village was barely over one acre, less than half the paddy-land judged necessary to provide a minimum standard of living to a family of four. Ten families are entirely without land and just over half Sedaka's households have incomes below the government-established poverty line. At the other end of the stratification the ten best-off households own over half the paddy-land held by villagers and cultivate, on average, over eight acres. These households constitute the economic elite of the village. Those among them (seven) who belong to the dominant Malay party (UMNO) dominate the quietly contentious political life of the village.

For our purposes, the major change in the economic and social life of Sedaka during the past decade was the beginning of double-cropping in 1971 and the mechanisation of the paddy harvest which came in its wake. Double-cropping, by itself, was something of a boon to virtually all strata of the village; landlords got double rents, owner-operators and tenants increased their annual profits, and even the roughly 28 families who depended on field labour for a substantial share of their income prospered as never before, transplanting and harvesting two crops. In a brief period of euphoria, homes were repaired and rebuilt, heads of households who had left earlier to find work elsewhere in the off-season found they could remain at home, and everyone had enough rice to feed their family the year round. Other consequences of double-cropping were, however, working to undermine the gains made by poorer villagers and they were decisively compounded by the introduction of combine-harvesters.

In 1975, virtually all the paddy in Muda was cut and threshed by hand. By 1980, huge western-style combines costing nearly M$200,000 and owned by syndicates of businessmen, were harvesting roughly 80 per cent of the rice crop. If it is hard to imagine the visual impact on the peasantry of this mind-boggling technological leap from sickles and threshing tubs to clanking behemoths with 32-foot cutting bars, it is not so hard to calculate their impact on the distribution of rural income. Paddy wage-labour receipts have been reduced by nearly half and transplanting remains the only major operation which still requires manual labour. The losses in income have, of course, been greatest among those most in need: smallholders, marginal tenants, and above all landless wage labourers. If the impact of mechanisation is added to the effects of stagnant paddy price for producers, rising input costs and rising consumer prices, the poorest half of Sedaka's households has lost nearly all of their original gains from double-cropping. Income distribution, meanwhile, has worsened appreciably as the gains of double-cropping have gone largely to the big farmers who own most of the land and local capital.

As with many technological changes, the secondary effects of combine-harvesting have been at least as important as its primary effects. To reduce what is a very complex story to its barest essentials, the following major consequences of combine-harvesting may be noted:[12]

(1) It virtually eliminated gleaning by grinding up the stalks which were previously left beside the threshing tubs. Gleaning had been a subsidiary food for many poor village families.
(2) It favoured the substitution of broadcast sowing for hand transplanting since the machine could more easily harvest paddy sown broadcast and of uneven height and maturity. By 1980 nearly half the paddy acreage was sown in this fashion thus eliminating that much employment for hand transplanting.
(3) It greatly reduced the demand for harvest labour thereby allowing a reduction in the effective wage-rate for the employment still available.
(4) It made it easier for larger landowners inside and outside the village to dismiss the tenants they had previously rented to and resume cultivation themselves by hiring machine services.
(5) It created a new class of wealthy, entrepreneurial leasehold tenants willing and able to rent in large tracts for many seasons at a time, paying the advance rent in a lump sum.

The transformations in paddy-growing since 1971 have not only resulted in the relative impoverishment of poorer villagers but also in their *marginalisation* so far as production relations are concerned. Until even 1975 rich landlords and farmers had more paddy-land than they could cultivate alone; they needed tenants, ploughing services, transplanters, reapers, and threshers. To ensure a reliable supply of labour it was common for better-off villagers to 'cultivate' the goodwill of their labour force as well as their land. They did this by giving occasional feasts, by extending *zakat* (the Islamic tithe) bonuses to harvest labourers, by small loans or gifts, and by socially tactful behaviour. Now, the well-to-do have little need to take on the poor as tenants or labourers. Correspondingly, they have little incentive to continue to cultivate their goodwill and the marginalisation of the poor is reflected in a much remarked decline in feast giving, in *zakat* and charity, and in overt respect flowing from the rich to the poor.

Obstacles to Open, Collective Resistance

Despite the economic reverses experienced by Sedaka's poor, despite the deteriorating quality of class relations evident behind the scenes, there have been no striking instances of overt class conflict. The reasons why this public silence should prevail are worth mentioning briefly precisely because they are, I believe, common to so many contexts of agrarian class relations as to suggest that the resistance we shall find here is the rule and not the exception. The situation the poor confront in Sedaka and on the Muda Plain is, after all, part of the ubiquitous and undramatic struggle against the effects of capitalist development in the countryside; the loss of access to the means of production (proletarianisation), the loss of work (marginalisation) and income, and the loss of what little respect and recognised social claims that went with their previous status. Most readings of the history of capitalist development, or simply a glance at the odds in this context, would indicate that this struggle is a lost cause. It may well be just that. If so, the poor peasantry of Sedaka finds itself in numerous and distinguished historical company. The *quiet* resistance of the victims in this case may be traced to two sets of reasons: one concerns the nature of the changes confronted by the poor as well as the nature of their community while another concerns the effects of repression.

Forms of resistance in Sedaka reflect the conditions and constraints under which they are generated. If they are open, they are rarely collective, and, if they are collective, they are rarely open. Here the analogy with small-scale, defensive, guerrilla skirmishes is once again appropriate. The encounters seldom amount to more than 'incidents'. The results are usually inconclusive, and the perpetrators move under cover of darkness or anonymity, melting back into the 'civilian' population for protective cover.

Perhaps the most important 'given' that structures the options open to Sedaka's poor is simply the nature of the changes which they have experienced. Some varieties of change, other things being equal, are more explosive than others – more likely to provoke open, collective defiance. In this category we might place those massive and sudden changes which decisively destroy nearly all the routines of daily life and, at the same time, threaten the livelihood of much of the population. Here in Sedaka, however, most of the changes that constitute the green revolution have been experienced as a series of *piecemeal* shifts in tenure and technique. As painful as the changes were, they tended to come gradually and to affect only a small minority of villagers at any one time. When landlords decided to resume cultivation themselves or to lease (*pajak*) their land to wealthy commercial operators, only a few tenants were threatened at a time and their difficulties at first seemed an individual misfortune rather than a general trend. Much the same can be said for the raising of rents and for the substitution of broadcasting for transplanting. The screws were turned piecemeal and at varying speeds so that the victims were never more than a handful at a time. In this case as in others, each landlord or farmer insisting on the change represented a *particular* situation confronting one or, at most, a few individuals.

The only exception to this pattern was the introduction of combine-harvesting and, as we shall see, it provoked the nearest thing to open, collective defiance. Even in this case, however, the impact was not instantaneous, nor was it without a certain ambiguity for many in the village. For the first two seasons the economic impact on the poor was noticeable but not devastating. Middle peasants were genuinely torn between the advantage of getting their crop in quickly and the loss of wage earning for themselves or their children. At no single moment did combine-harvesting represent a collective threat to the livelihood of a solid majority of villagers.

Another striking characteristic of the agricultural transformation in Kedah – one that serves very powerfully to defuse class-conflict is the fact that it simply removes the poor from the productive process rather than directly exploiting them. One after another, the large farmers and landlords in the Muda Scheme have *eliminated* terrains of potential struggle over the distribution of the harvest and profits from paddy-growing. In place of the struggle over piece-rates for cutting and threshing, there is now only a single payment to the machine-broker. In place of negotiations over transplanting costs, there is the option of broadcasting the seed and avoiding the conflict altogether. In place of tense and contentious disputes over the timing and level of rents there is increasingly the alternative of hiring the machines and farming oneself or of leasing to an outsider for a lump sum. The changes themselves, of course – dismissing a tenant, switching to the machines – are not so simple to put across. But once they have been put across, the ex-tenant or ex-wage labourer simply ceases to be relevant; there is no further season-by-season struggle because the poor have become redundant. Once the connection and the struggle in the realm of production has been severed it is a simple matter also to sever the connection – and the struggle – in the realm of ritual, charity, and even sociability. This central aspect of the green revolution, by itself, goes a long way toward accounting for the relative absence, here and elsewhere, of mass violence. If the profits of the green revolution had depended on squeezing more from the tenants, rather than dismissing them, or extracting more work for less pay from labourers, the consequences for class conflict would surely have been far more dramatic. As it is, the profits from double-cropping depend far less on exploiting the poor than on ignoring and replacing them. Class conflict, like any conflict, is played out on a site – the threshing floor, the assembly line, the place where piece-rates or rents are settled – where vital interests are at stake. What double-cropping in Muda has achieved is a rather massive bulldozing of the sites where class conflict has historically occurred.

A related obstacle to open protest is already implicit in the piecemeal impact of double-cropping. The impact of each of the changes we have discussed is mediated by the very complex and overlapping class structure of Sedaka. There are well-off tenants and very poor tenants; there are land-lords who are (or whose children are) also tenants and labourers; there are smallholders who need wage-work to survive but also hire the combines. Thus each of the important shifts in tenure and production creates not only victims and beneficiaries but also a substantial strata whose interests are not so easily discerned. Sedaka is not Morelos where a poor and largely undifferentiated peasantry confronted a common enemy in the sugar plan-tation. It is in fact only in comparatively rare circumstances where the class structure of the countryside was such as to produce either a decisive single cleavage or a nearly uniform response to external pressure. The situation in Sedaka is, I believe, the more common one. The very complexity of the local class structure militates against collective opinion and, hence, collective action on most issues.

The obstacles to collective action presented by the local class structure are compounded by other cleavages and alliances which cut across class. These are the familiar links of kinship, faction, patronage, and ritual ties that muddy the class waters in virtually *any* small community. Nearly without exception, they operate to the advantage of the richer farmers by creating a relationship of dependence that restrains the prudent poor man or woman from acting in class terms.

Lest one gain the impression from the foregoing that the obstacles to class conflict in Sedaka are entirely a matter of the complex local stratification and the piecemeal character of changes in production relations, I hasten to add that repression and the fear of repression are very much involved as well. Here it is sufficient simply to note that popular efforts to halt or impede the growth of combine-harvesting occurred in a climate of fear generated by local elites, by the police, by the 'Special Branch' internal security forces, by a pattern of political arrests and intimidation. Open political activity was both rare and firmly repressed. A popular demonstration in Alor Star, the state capital, in early 1980, demanding an increase in the farm-gate paddy price was greeted with arrests of many opposition figures, threats of de-tention, and promises of even more draconian action if the protests con-tinued. The fear of reprisal or arrest was mentioned explicitly by many as a reason for maintaining a low profile.

A final obstacle to open defiance might be called 'the duress of the quotidian'. The perspective I have in mind is best expressed in the words of Hassan, a poor man who was given less than the expected wage for filling paddy stacks. Asked why he said nothing to his wealthy employer, he replied, 'Poor people can't complain; when I'm sick or need work, I may have to ask him again. I am angry in my heart.' What is operating here is something which Marx appropriately termed 'the dull compulsion of economic relations' – a compulsion which can occur only against a background of expected repression [*Marx, 1970*:737]. Lacking any realistic possibility, for the time being, of directly and collectively redressing their situation, the village poor have little choice but to adjust, as best they can, to the circumstances they confront daily. Tenants may bitterly resent the rent they must pay for their small plot, but they must pay it or lose the land; the near-landless may deplore the loss of wage-work, but they must scramble for the few opportunities available; they may harbour deep animosities toward the clique which dominates village politics, but they must act with circumspection if they wish to benefit from any of the small advantages which that clique can confer.

At least two aspects of this grudging, pragmatic adaptation to the realities merit emphasis. The first is that it does not rule out *certain* forms of resistance, although it surely sets limits that only the foolhardy would transgress. The second is that it is, above all, pragmatic; it does not at all imply normative consent to those realities. To understand this is simply to grasp what is, in all likelihood, the situation for most subordinate classes historically. They struggle under conditions which are largely not of their own making and their pressing material needs necessitate something of a daily accommodation to those conditions. If much of the 'conforming' day-to-day public behaviour of the poor in Sedaka reflects the realities of immediate power relations, there is surely no need to assume that it drives from some symbolic hegemony, let alone, consensus. The duress of the quotidian is quite sufficient.[12]

The Effort to Stop the Combine

The introduction of combine-harvesting, the most sudden and devastating of the changes associated with double-cropping, also stirred the most active resistance. This resistance went well beyond arguments about its efficiency, the complaints over lost wages, and the slander directed against those who hired the combine. Throughout the rice bowl of Kedah there were efforts physically to obstruct its entry into the field, incidents of arson and sabotage, and widespread attempts to organise 'strikes' of transplanters against those who first hired the machine. All of these actions ultimately failed to prevent the mechanisation of the paddy harvest, although they undoubtedly limited and delayed it somewhat.

Sabotage and obstruction of the combines began as early as 1970 when a few small experimental machines were used in field trials. It was only in 1976, however, that large-scale commercial machine harvesting – and therefore widespread acts of vengence – began. Officials of the Muda Agricultural Development Authority chose to speak simply of 'vandalism'. Batteries were removed from the machines and thrown into irrigation ditches, carburettors and other vital parts such as distributors and air filters were smashed; sand and mud were put into the gas tank, and various objects (stones, wire, nails) were thrown into the augers. At least one combine was burned. A small group of men awoke the night watchman sleeping in the cab, ordered him down, and, using the kerosene they had brought along, set the machine on fire. In a good many villages, veiled rumours of possible violence persuaded many large farmers to hesitate before hiring a combine. Such tactics in one village actually prevented any machine harvesting for three full seasons. Two aspects of this sabotage and associated threats deserve particular emphasis. First, it was clear that the goal of the saboteurs was not simple theft, for nothing was actually stolen. Second, *all* of the sabotage was carried out at night by individuals or small groups acting anonymously. They were, furthermore, shielded by their fellow villagers who, if they knew who was involved, claimed total ignorance when the police came to investigate. As a result, no prosecutions were ever made. The practice of posting a night watchman to guard the combine dates from these early trials.

At about the same time there were the beginnings of a quiet but more collective effort by women to bring pressure to bear on the farmers who hired the machines. Men and women – often from the same family – had, of course, each lost work to the combine, but it was only the women who still had any real bargaining power. They were, for the time being, still in control of transplanting. The group of women (*kumpulan share*) who reaped a farmer's land was typically the same group that had earlier transplanted the same field. They were losing roughly half their seasonal earnings and they understandably resented transplanting a crop for a farmer who would use the combine at harvest time. Thus, in Sedaka and, it appears, throughout much of the Muda region, such women resolved to organise a boycott (*boikot*) that would deny transplanting services to their employers who hired the combine.

Three of the five 'share groups' in Sedaka made some attempts to enforce such a boycott. Each group was composed of anywhere from six to nine village women. The remaining two groups did not participate but they refused to help break the boycott by planting for any farmer who was being 'boycotted' by one of the other three gangs. Why the groups of Rosni, Rokiah, and Mariam took the initiative is not entirely clear. They are composed of women from families which are, on average, slightly poorer than those in the remaining two groups, but only slightly. If we rely on local explanations for the pattern of resistance, the consensus is that Rosni and Rokiah depend heavily on wage labour to support their families and are, at the same time, 'courageous' (*berani*).[14]

The boycott actually represented a very cautious form of resistance. At *no* time was there ever an open confrontation between a farmer who used the combine and his transplanters. Instead, the anonymous and indirect approach of rumours and hints (*cara sembunyi tau*) with which we are familiar was employed. The women *let it be known* through intermediaries that the group was not pleased (*tak puas hati*) with the loss of harvest work and would be reluctant (*segan*) to transplant the fields of those who had hired the combine the previous season. They also 'let it be known' that when and if a combine broke down in the course of the harvest, a farmer who then wanted to get his crop in by hand could not count on his old workers to bail him out.

When it came time, at the beginning of the irrigated season of 1977, to make good this threat, circumspection again prevailed. None of the three groups refused outright to transplant paddy for those who had harvested with the combine in the previous season. Rather, they delayed; the head of the share group would tell the offending farmer that they were busy and could not get to his land just yet. Only a dozen or so farmers had used the combine the previous season, so the share groups had a good deal of work to occupy them just transplanting the crops of those who had not mechanised. The transplanters thus kept their options open; they avoided a direct refusal to transplant which would have provoked an open break. Fully abreast of the rumours of a boycott, the farmers who had been put off became increasingly anxious as their nursery paddy (*semai*) was passing its prime and as they feared their crop might not be fully mature before the scheduled date for shutting off the supply of water. Their state of mind was not improved by the sight of their neighbour's newly transplanted fields next to their own vacant plots.

After more than two weeks of this war of nerves – this seeming boycott that never fully announced itself – six farmers 'let it be known' indirectly that they were arranging for outside labourers to come and transplant their crops. The six were large farmers by village standards, cultivating a total of nearly 70 acres. They claimed in their defence, that they had pressed for a firm commitment for a transplanting date from their local share group and, only after being put off again, had they moved. At this point, the boycott collapsed. Each of the three share groups was faced with defections as women feared that this transplanting work would be permanently lost to outsiders. They hastily sent word that they would begin transplanting the land in question within the next few days. Three of the six farmers cancelled their arrangements with the outside gangs while the other three went ahead either because they felt it was too late to cancel or because they wished to teach the women a lesson. Transplanters came from the town of Yan (just outside the irrigation scheme) and from Singkir and Merbuk, further away. One farmer, Haji Salim, using his considerable political influence, arranged with local authorities to bring in a gang of Thai transplanters – a practice he has continued and for which he is bitterly resented.

The brief and abortive attempt to stop the combine by collective action was the subject of demoralised or self-satisfied post-mortems, depending in which side of the fence one happened to be. Aside from the pleasure or disappointment expressed, the post-mortems converged on the inevitability of the outcome. Even those with most to lose from mechanisation had realised that if their bluff were called, it would be nearly impossible to move beyond talk and vague threats. They agreed sadly that 'it was just talk and we planted anyway. What could we do?' To have continued to refuse to transplant once outside labourers had been brought in would have meant further jeopardising an already precarious livelihood. The futility of such a refusal was more than once characterised by the use of a Malay saying closely approximating the English 'cutting off your nose to spite your face'.[15] Or as the villager who became the local machine-broker put it: "The poor have to work anyway; they can't hold out." A healthy interest in survival required them to swallow their pride and return to work. In fact, the possibility of this outcome was implicit in the indirectness with which the boycott was conducted; an open confrontation and boycott would have meant burning their bridges behind them. Instead they left open an avenue of retreat. In terms of public discourse the boycott was a non-event; it was never openly declared; it was thus never *openly* defeated; the use of delays and barely plausible excuses meant that the intention to boycott itself could be disavowed.

The goals of the attempted 'strike' in Sedaka and innumerable other villages on the Kedah Plain were ambitious.[16] The women aimed at nothing less than blocking a momentous change in production relations. Their means, as we have seen, however, were modest and disguised. And while they certainly failed to stop the mechanisation of the harvest, their attempt has not been completely futile. There is little doubt that combine-harvesting would have been adopted more rapidly had it not been for the resistance. For poor villagers living at the margin the time gained has proven vital. Five years after the introduction of combines there are still five or six farmers who hire hand labour for some or all of their paddy harvest because, they say, their neighbours need the work. There is little doubt that they have been influenced by the underground campaign of slander and defamation waged against those who invariably hire the machines.

The Theft of Paddy: Routine Resistance

The attempt to halt combine-harvesting, while hardly the stuff of high drama, was surely out of the ordinary. It took place against a rarely noticed background of routine resistance over wages, tenancy, rents, and the distribution of paddy that is a permanent feature of life in Sedaka and in any stratified agrarian setting. A close examination of this realm of struggle exposes an implicit form of local trade unionism which is reinforced both by mutuality among the poor and by a considerable amount of theft and violence against property. None of this activity poses a fundamental threat to the basic structure of agrarian inequalities, either materially or symbolically. What it does represent, however, is a constant process of testing and renegotiation of production relations between classes. On both sides – landlord–tenant, farmer–wage-labourer – there is a never-ending attempt to seize each small advantage and press it home, to probe the limits of the existing relationships, to see precisely what can be got away with at the margin, and to include this margin as a part of an accepted, or at least tolerated, territorial claim. Over the past decade the flow of this frontier battle has, of course, rather consistently favoured the fortunes of the large farmers and landlords. They have not only swallowed large pieces of the territory defended by wage-workers and tenants but, in doing so, they have thereby reduced (through marginalisation) the perimeter along which the struggle continues. Even along this reduced perimeter, however, there is constant pressure exerted by those who hope to regain at least a small patch of what they have grudgingly lost. The resisters require little explicit co-ordination to conduct this struggle, for the simple imperative of making a tolerable living is enough to make them dig in their heels.

The dimensions and conduct of this more 'routine' resistance could fill volumes. For our purposes here, however, most of the basic issues raised by resistance of this kind can be seen in a particularly 'popular' form it takes: the theft of paddy.[17] Rural theft by itself is unremarkable, it is nearly a permanent feature of stratified agrarian life whenever and wherever the state and its agents are insufficient to control it. When such theft takes on the dimensions of a struggle in which property rights are being contested, however, it may become an essential element of any careful analysis of class relations.

The amount of paddy stolen over a single season, while not large as a proportion of the total harvest, is alarming to the large farmers and, what is more, they believe that it is growing. No firm statistics are available, of course, but I made an effort to record all the losses of paddy reported to me during the 1979–80 main season. By far the largest category of thefts were whole gunny sacks of threshed paddy left in the fields overnight during the harvest. These are listed below.

REPORTED THEFTS OF THRESHED PADDY BY THE SACK
IN MAIN SEASON 1979–80

Farmer	Reported Loss gunny sack(s)
Shahnon	1
Haji Kadir	1
Samat	1
Abu Hassan	2
Ghani Lebai Mat	1
Amin	2
Tok Long	2
Idris	1
Lebai Pendek	2
Fadzil	1
Total	14

(Approximate cash value = M$532.)

To this total one must add paddy that was spirited away in other ways. At least four gunny sacks of paddy drying in the sun on mats disappeared. Two very well-off farmers each lost a gunny sack which was stored beneath their respective houses. Something like the same quantity of paddy was reported stolen from rice barns (*jelapang*) in the course of the season.[18] A small amount of paddy was reported taken on the stalk from the fields. How much is difficult to say, but the quantity is not substantial; villagers point out that the sound of threshing and the disposal of the straw would present a problem for the thief, while the rich claim that thieves are too lazy actually to put themselves to the trouble of threshing. Finally, a thorough accounting of paddy thefts would have to include some estimate of the grain which threshers are said to stuff into their pockets and inside their shirts at the end of the day's work. Such pilfering is 'winked at' by most farmers and I have made no attempt to calculate how much paddy is appropriated in this way during the harvest.

Certain facts about the pattern of theft are worth noting. The first is that, with the exception of two farmers who are only modestly well-off, all of the victims are among the wealthiest third of Sedaka's households. This may indicate nothing more than the obvious fact that such households are likely to have more paddy lying in the field at harvest time and that smallholders, who can ill afford the loss, take pains to get the threshed paddy to their house quickly. It is certainly true that large farmers with plots far from their houses that cannot be threshed (and hence stored) in a single day are the most prone to such losses. But here it is significant to realise that the pattern of theft is an artifact of the pattern of property relations prevailing in Sedaka. The rich, by and large, possess what is worth taking while the poor have the greatest incentive to take it. No one doubts either that poor men, *local* poor men at that, are responsible for the vast majority of the paddy thefts.

The total amount of paddy stolen, perhaps 20 to 25 gunny sacks, is less than one-hundredth of the paddy harvested in a season by all village farmers. By this measure, the losses are fairly trivial and are borne largely by those who produce a substantial surplus. If, however, we measure its significance by what it may add to the food supply of a few of the poorest families in the village, then it may be quite significant. It is of some interest that these 20 to 25 gunny sacks of paddy are more than half the quantity of grain given *voluntarily* by farmers as an Islamic tithe (*zakat peribadi*) after the harvest. The comparison is apt precisely because I twice heard poor men refer smilingly to paddy thefts (*curian padi*) as '*zakat peribadi* that one takes on his own' (*zakat peribadi, angkat sindiri*). This evidence is certainly not conclusive – but it is entirely possible that some of the poor, at any rate, consider such acts not so much as theft but as the appropriation of what they feel entitled to by earlier custom – a kind of forcible poor tax to replace the gifts and wages they no longer receive. In this connection, two other items of circumstantial evidence are relevant. Only one of the farmers who lost paddy (Samat) was among those ever praised by the poor for their reluctance to hire the combine, while all the others have used the machine whenever possible. There is also some indication that paddy thefts may be used as a sanction by disgruntled labourers. Thus Sukur once told me that farmers were careful to hire the threshers they had customarily invited since anyone who was omitted might, in his anger, steal paddy from the fields. If, indeed, the theft of paddy has a certain element of popular justice to it, the scope for such resistance has been considerably narrowed by the use of combines which make it possible to gather and store (or sell) a farmer's entire crop in a single day. Combines thus not only eliminate hand reaping, hand threshing, in-field transport, and gleaning; they also tend to eliminate theft.

The attitude of wealthy farmers toward such thefts is a combination of anger, as one might expect, and also *fear*. Haji Kadir, for example, was furious enough over his loss to consider spending the following night in the fields guarding his paddy with his shotgun. He did not follow through because he reasoned that the mere rumour that he might lie in wait would be sufficient to deter any thief. The element of fear can be gauged, in part, by the fact that no police report of a paddy theft has ever been made in Sedaka. Wealthy farmers explained to me that if they made such a report and named a suspect, word would get around quickly and they feared that they would then become a target for more thefts. Haji Kadir, the wealthiest farmer in the village, once spied someone stealing a gunny sack at night from a neighbour's field. Not only did he fail to intervene to stop the theft, but he would not even inform his neighbour, even though he was certain about the identity of the thief. When I asked him why, he replied that the thief had seen him too, would know he was the informer, and would steal his paddy next. In an earlier season, Mat Sarif lost two gunny sacks but told me that he did not *want* to know who did it. Old and quite frail, he added simply, 'I'm afraid of being killed (*takut mampus*)'. For a handful of the more daring village poor, it would appear that something of a small balance of terror has been struck that permits such limited pilfering to continue.[19]

Other forms of resistance by the poor of Sedaka vary in particulars but not in general contour. One distinguishing mark of virtually all resistance in Sedaka is the relative absence of any open confrontation between classes. Where resistance is collective, it is carefully circumspect; where it is an individual or small group attack on property, it is anonymous and usually nocturnal.[20] By its calculated prudence and secrecy it preserves, for the most part, the on-stage theatre of power which dominates public life in Sedaka. Any intention to storm the stage can be disavowed and options are consciously kept open. Deference and conformity, though rarely cringing, continue to be the public posture of the poor. For all that, however, backstage one can clearly make out a continuous testing of limits.

Resistance in Sedaka has virtually nothing that one expects to find in the typical history of rural conflict. There are no riots, no demonstrations, no arson, no organised social banditry, no open violence. The resistance we have discovered is not linked to any larger outside political movements, ideologies, or revolutionary cadres – although it is clear that similar struggles have been occurring in virtually any village in the region. The sorts of activities found here *require* little co-ordination, let alone political organisation, though they might benefit from it. They are, in short, forms of

struggle that are almost entirely indigeneous to the village sphere. Providing
that we are careful about the use of the term, these activities might appropriately be called *primitive* resistance. The use of 'primitive' does not imply, as
Hobsbawm does, that they are somehow backward and destined to give way
to more sophisticated ideologies and tactics.[21] It implies only that such forms
of resistance are the nearly permanent, continuous, daily strategies of
subordinate rural classes under difficult conditions. At times of crisis or
momentous political change they may be complemented by other forms of
struggle which are more opportune. They are unlikely, however, to disappear altogether so long as the rural social structure remains exploitative
and inequitable. They are the stubborn bedrock upon which other forms of
resistance may grow and they are likely to persist *after* such other forms have
failed or produced, in turn, a new pattern of inequity.

III. WHAT COUNTS AS RESISTANCE

But can the activities we have described and others like them be seen as
resistance? Can we call a boycott that was never even announced, class
resistance? Why should we consider the theft of a few gunny sacks of paddy
as a form of class resistance; there was no collective action nor was there any
open challenge to the system of property and domination. Many of the same
questions could be raised about gossip and character assassination which is
one of the principal means by which the poor of Sedaka consistently try to
influence the behaviour of the well-to-do.

  As a first approximation, I propose the following definition for peasant
class resistance – one that would include many of the activities we have
discussed. The purpose behind this definition is not to settle these important
issues by fiat, but rather to highlight the conceptual problems we face in
understanding resistance and to make what I believe to be a plausible case
for a rather wide understanding of the term.

> Lower class resistance among peasants is any act(s) by member(s) of
> the class that is (are) intended either to mitigate or to deny claims (e.g.
> rents, taxes, deference) made on that class by superordinate classes
> (e.g. landlords, the state, owners of machinery, moneylenders) or to
> advance its own claims (e.g. work, land, charity, respect) vis-à-vis
> these superordinate classes.

Three aspects of the definition merit brief comment. First, there is no
requirement that resistance take the form of collective action. Second – and
this is a very nettlesome issue – intentions are built into the definition. We
will return to this problem again but, for the moment, the formulation allows
for the fact that many intended acts of resistance may backfire and produce
consequences that were entirely unanticipated. Finally, the definition re-
cognises what we might call symbolic or ideological resistance (for example,
gossip, slander, rejecting imposed categories, the withdrawal of deference)
as an integral part of class-based resistance.

The problem of intentions is enormously complex and not simply because the as-yet-unapprehended paddy thieves of our earlier example are unwilling to be identified, let alone to discuss their intentions once they have been located. The larger issue has to do with our tendency to think of resistance as actions that involve at least some short-run individual or collective sacrifice in order to bring about a longer-range collective gain. The immediate losses of a strike, a boycott, or even the refusal to compete with other members of one's class for land or work are obvious cases in point. When it comes to acts like theft, however, we encounter a combination of immediate individual gain and what *may* be resistance. How are we to judge which of the two purposes is uppermost or decisive? What is at stake here is not a petty definitional matter but rather the interpretation of a whole range of actions which seem to me to lie historically at the core of everyday class relations. The English poacher in the eighteenth century *may* have been resisting gentry's claim to property in wild game, but he was just as surely interested in rabbit stew. The South-east Asian peasant who hid his rice and possessions from the tax collector may have been protesting high taxes, but he was just as surely seeing to it that his family would have enough rice until the next harvest. The peasant conscript who deserted the army may have been a war resister, but he was just as surely saving his own skin by fleeing the front. Which of these inextricably fused motives are we to take as paramount? Even if we were *able* to ask the actors in question and even if they could reply candidly, it is not at all clear that they would be able to make a clear determination.

Students of slavery, who have looked into this matter most closely, if only because such forms of self-help were frequently the only option open, have tended to discount such actions as 'real' resistance for three reasons. All three of these reasons figure in Gerald Mullin's analysis of slave 'rebelliousness'.

> In assessing these observable differences in slave behavior, scholars usually ask whether a particular rebellious style represented resistance to slavery's abuses or *real* resistance to slavery itself. When slave behavior is examined in light of its political content, the most menial workers, the field slaves, fare badly. Speaking generally, their 'laziness,' boondoggling, and pilferage represented a *limited*, perhaps *self-indulgent* type of rebelliousness. Their reactions to unexpected abuses or to sudden changes in plantation routine were at most only *token* acts against slavery. But the plantation slaves' *organized* and systematic schemes to obstruct the plantation's workings – their *persistent* acts of attrition against crops and stores, and *cooperative* night-time robberies that sustained the black-markets – were more 'political' in their *consequences* and represented resistance to slavery itself [*Mullin*, 1972: 35; emphasis added].

Although Eugene Genovese's position on this issue differs in some important particulars, he too insists on distinguishing between 'pre-political' forms of resistance and more significant resistance to the regime of slavery. The distinction for him, as the following quote indicates, lies in both the realm of consequences *and* the real of intentions.

> Strictly speaking, only insurrection represented political action, which some choose to define as the only genuine resistance since it alone directly challenged the power of the regime. From that point of view, those activities which others call 'day to day resistance to slavery' – stealing, lying, dissembling, shirking, murder, infanticide, suicide, arson – qualify at best as prepolitical and at worst as apolitical .... But 'day to day resistance to slavery' generally implied accommodation and made no sense except on the assumption of an accepted status quo the norm of which, as perceived or defined by the slaves, had been violated [*Genovese*, 1974: 598].

Combining these overlapping perspectives, the result is something of a dichotomy between *real* resistance on the one hand and 'token', incidental, or even epiphenomenal 'activities' on the other. 'Real' resistance, it is argued, is (a) organised, systematic, and co-operative, (b) principled or selfless, (c) has revolutionary consequences, and/or (d) embodies ideas or intentions that negate the basis of domination itself. 'Token', incidental, or epiphenomenal 'activities' by contrast are (a) unorganised, unsystematic and individual, (b) opportunistic and 'self-indulgent', (c) have no revolutionary consequences, and/or (d) imply, in their intention or logic, an accommodation with the system of domination. Now these distinctions are important for any analysis which has as its objective the attempt to delineate the various forms of resistance and to show how they are related to one another and to the form of domination in which they occur. My quarrel is rather with the contention that the latter forms are, ultimately, trivial or inconsequential, while only the former can be said to constitute real resistance. This position, in my view, fundamentally misconstrues the very basis of the economic and political struggle conducted daily by subordinate classes – not only slaves, but peasants and workers as well – in repressive settings. It is based on an ironic combination of both Leninist and bourgeois assumptions of what constitutes political action. The first three of the paired comparisons will be addressed here. The final issue of whether intentions are accommodationist or revolutionary would require a lengthy, separate analysis.

Let us begin with the question of actions which are 'self-indulgent', individual, and unorganised. Embedded in the logic of Genovese and, especially, of Mullins, is the assumption that such acts intrinsically lack revolutionary *consequences*. This *may* often be the case, but it is also the case that there is hardly a modern revolution that can be successfully explained without reference to precisely such acts when they take place on a massive scale. Take again the matter of military desertion and the role it has played in revolutions. The Russian Revolution is a striking case in point.

Growing desertions from the largely peasant rank-and-file of the Tsarist army in the summer of 1917 were a major and indispensable part of the revolutionary process in at least two respects. First, they were responsible for the collapse of the main institution of repression of the Tsarist state – an institution which had earlier, in 1905, put down another revolutionary upheaval. Second, the deserters contributed directly to the revolutionary process in the countryside by participating in the seizures of land throughout the core provinces of European Russia. And it is abundantly clear that the haemorrhage in the Tsarist forces was largely 'self-indulgent', 'unorganised', and 'individual' – although thousands and thousands of individuals threw down their arms and headed home.[23] The attack into Austria had been crushed with huge losses of troops and officers; the ration of bread had been reduced and 'fast-days' inaugurated at the front; the soldiers knew, moreover, that if they stayed at the front they might miss the chance to gain from the land seizures breaking out in the countryside.[24] Desertion offered the peasant conscripts the chance of saving their skins and of returning home where bread and, now land, were available. The risks were minimal since discipline in the army had dissolved. One can hardly imagine a set of more 'self-indulgent' goals. But it was just such self-indulgent ends, acted on by unorganised masses of 'self-demobilized' peasant soldiers which made the Revolution possible [*Carr*, 1966: 103].

The disintegration of the Tsarist army is but one of many instances where the aggregation of a host of petty, self-interested acts of insubordination or desertion, with no revolutionary intent, have created a revolutionary situation. The dissolution of the Nationalist armies of Chaing Kai-shek in 1948 or of Saigon's army in 1975 could no doubt be analysed among similar lines. And long before the final debacle, acts of insubordination and non-compliance in each army – as well as in the US Army serving in Vietnam, it should be added – had set sharp limits on what the counter-revolutionary forces could expect and require of their own rank-and-file.[25] Resistance of this kind is, of course, not a monopoly of the counter-revolution as George Washington and Emiliano Zapata, among others, discovered. We can imagine that the eminently personal logic of Pedro Martinez, a some-time soldier with the Zapatista forces, was not markedly different from that of the Tsarist soldiers leaving the front.

> That's where [battle of Tizapán] I finally had it. The battle was something awful! The shooting was tremendous! It was a completely bloody battle, three days and three nights. But I took it for one day and then I left. I quit the army ... I said to myself, 'It's time now I got back to my wife, to my little children. I'm getting out.' ... I said to myself, 'No, my family comes first and they are starving. Now I'm leaving.' [*Lewis*, 1964: 102].

The refreshing candor of Pedro Martinez serves to remind us that there is no necessary relationship between the banality of the act of self-preservation and family obligations on the one hand and the banality of the consequences of such acts. Multiplied many times, acts that could in no way be considered 'political' may have the most massive consequences for states as well as armies.

The issue here is by no means confined to desertion from armies which has been chosen only as a diagnostic illustration. It applies with nearly equal force to the tradition of peasant flight, to theft, to the shirking of corvée labour; the consequences of such acts of self-help may be all out of proportion to the trifling intentions of the actors themselves.

While the consequences of peasant, self-serving behaviour are essential to any larger analysis of class relations or of the state, I do *not* wish to argue that resistance should be defined with reference to its consequences alone. Such a view runs into formidable difficulties of its own, if for no other reason than the 'law of unintended consequences.' Any definition of resistance thus requires at least *some* reference to the intentions of the actors. The problem with existing concepts of resistance is therefore not that they must inevitably deal with intentions and meaning as well as with consequences. Rather, the problem lies in what is a misleading, sterile, and sociologically naive insistence upon distinguishing 'self-indulgent', individual acts on the one hand from presumably 'principled', selfless, collective actions on the other and excluding the former from the category of *real* resistance. To insist on such distinctions as a means of comparing forms of resistance and their consequences is one thing; but to use them as the basic criteria to determine what constitutes resistance is to miss the very wellsprings of peasant politics.

It is no coincidence that the cries of 'bread', 'land', and 'no taxes' that so often lie at the core of peasant rebellion are each joined to the basic material survival needs of the peasant household. Nor should it be anything more than a commonplace that everyday peasant politics and everyday peasant resistance (and also, of course, everyday compliance) flows from these same fundamental material needs. We need assume no more than an understandable desire on the part of the peasant household to survive – to ensure its physical safety, to ensure its food supply, to ensure its necessary cash income – to identify the source of its resistance to the claims of press gangs, tax collectors, landlords, and employers.

To ignore the self-interested element in peasant resistance is to ignore the determinate context, not only of peasant politics, but of most lower class politics. It is precisely the fusion of self-interest and resistance that is the vital force animating the resistance of peasants and proletarians. When a peasant hides part of his crop to avoid paying taxes, he is both filling his stomach and depriving the state of grain.[26] When a peasant soldier deserts the army because the food is bad and his crops at home are ripe, he is both looking after himself and denying the state cannon fodder. When such acts are rare and isolated, they are of little interest; but when they become a consistent pattern (even though uncoordinated, let alone organised) we are dealing with resistance. The intrinsic nature and, in one sense, the 'beauty' of much peasant resistance is that it often confers immediate and concrete advantages while at the same time denying resources to the appropriating classes *and* that it requires little or no manifest organisation. The stubbornness and force of such resistance flows directly from the fact that it is so firmly rooted in the shared material struggle experienced by a class.

To require of lower class resistance that it somehow be 'principled' or 'selfless' is not only a slander on the moral status of fundamental human needs. It is, more fundamentally, a misconstruction of the basis of class struggle which is, first and foremost, a struggle over the appropriation of work, production, property, and taxes. 'Bread-and-butter' issues are the essence of lower class politics and resistance. Consumption, from this perspective, is both the goal and the result of resistance and counter-resistance. As Utsa Patnaik has noted, 'consumption is nothing but the historically "necessary labor", the share of net output allowed to be retained by the petty producers as the outcome of their struggle with the surplus-appropriating classes' [1979: 398–9]. This is then the self-interested core of routine class struggle: the often defensive effort to mitigate or defeat appropriation. Petty thefts of grain or pilfering on the threshing floor may seem like trivial 'coping' mechanisms from one vantage point; but from a broader view of class relations, how the harvest is actually divided belongs at the centre.

A further advantage of a concept of resistance which begins with self-interested material needs is that it is far more in keeping with how 'class' is first experienced by the historical actors themselves. Here, I subscribe wholeheartedly to the judgement reached by E.P. Thompson on the basis of his own compelling analysis of working class history.

> In my view, far too much theoretical attention (much of it plainly a-historical) has been paid to 'class' and far too litle to 'class-struggle.' Indeed, class struggle is the prior, as well as the more universal, concept. To put it bluntly, classes do not exist as separate entities, look around, find an enemy class, and then start to struggle. On the contrary, people find themselves in a society structured in determined ways (crucially, but not exclusively, in productive relations), they experience exploitation (or the need to maintain power over those whom they exploit), they identify points of antagonistic interest, they commence to struggle around these issues and in the process of struggling they discover themselves as classes, they come to know this discovery as class-consciousness. Class and class consciousness are always the *last*, not the first, stage in the real historical process [1978: 149].

The inclination to dismiss 'individual' acts of resistance as insignificant and to reserve the term of 'resistance' for collective or organised action is as misguided as the emphasis on 'principled' action. The privileged status accorded organised movements, I suspect, flows from either of two political orientations: the one, essentially Leninist, which regards the only viable class action as that which is led by a vanguard party serving as a 'general-staff', the other more straightforwardly derived from a familiarity and preference for open, institutionalised politics as conducted in capitalist democracies. In either case, however, there is a misapprehension of the social and political circumstances within which peasant resistance is typically carried out.

The individual and often anonymous quality of much peasant resistance is, of course, eminently suited to the sociology of the class from which it arises. Being scattered in small communities and generally lacking the institutional means to act collectively, it is likely to employ those means of resistance which are local and require little co-ordination. Under special historical circumstances of overwhelming material deprivation, a breakdown in the institutions of repression, or the protection of political liberty (more rarely, all three) the peasantry can and has become an organised, political, mass movement. Such circumstances are, however, extremely rare and usually short-lived. In most places at most times these political options have simply been precluded. The penchant for forms of resistance that are individual and unobtrusive are not only what a Marxist might expect from petty commodity producers and rural labourers, but they also have certain advantages. Unlike hierarchical formal organisations, there is no centre, no leadership, no identifiable structure that can be co-opted or neutralised. What is lacking in terms of central co-ordination may be compensated for by flexibility and persistence. These forms of resistance will win no set-piece battles but they are admirably adopted to long-run campaigns of attrition.

If we are to confine our search for peasant resistance to formally organised activity we would search largely in vain, for in Malaysia as in many other Third World countries, such organisations are either absent or are the creations of officials and rural elites. We would simply miss much of what is happening. Formal political activity may be the norm for the elites, the intelligentsia, and the middle classes in the Third World as well as in the West, who have a near-monopoly of institutional skills and access, but it would be naive to expect that peasant resistance can or will normally take the same form.

Nor should we forget that the forms of peasant resistance are not just a product of the social ecology of the peasantry. The parameters of resistance are also set, in part, by the institutions of repression. To the extent that such institutions do their 'work' effectively, they may all but preclude any forms of resistance other than the individual, the informal, and the clandestine. Thus, it is perfectly legitimate – even important – to distinguish between various levels and forms of resistance: formal–informal, individual–collective, public–anonymous, those which challenge the system of domination – those which aim at marginal gains. But it should, at the same time, be made crystal clear that what we may actually be measuring in this enterprise is the level of repression which structures the options which are available. Depending on the circumstances they confront, peasants may oscillate from organised electoral activity to violent confrontations, to silent and anonymous acts of footdragging and theft. This oscillation may, in some cases, be due to changes in the social organisation of the peasantry, but it is as, if not more, likely to be due to changes in the level of repression. More than one peasantry has been brutally reduced from open, radical political activity at one moment to stubborn and sporadic acts of petty resistance at the next. If we allow ourselves to call only the former 'resistance', we simply allow the structure of domination to define for us what is resistance and what is not resistance.

Many of the forms of resistance we have been examining may be 'individual' actions, but this is not to say that they are uncoordinated. Here again, a concept of co-ordination derived from formal and bureaucratic settings is of little assistance in understanding actions in small communities with dense informal networks and rich, and historically deep, sub-cultures of resistance to outside claims. It is, for example, no exaggeration to say that much of the folk-culture of the peasant 'little tradition' amounts to a legitimation, or even a *celebration*, of precisely the kinds of evasive and cunning forms of resistance we have examined. In this and in other ways (for example, tales of bandits, peasant heroes, religious myths) the peasant sub-culture helps to underwrite dissimulation, poaching, theft, tax evasion, avoidance of conscription and so on. While folk-culture is not co-ordination in the formal sense, it often achieves a 'climate of opinion' which, in other more institutionalised societies, would require a public relations campaign. The striking thing about peasant society is the extent to which a whole range of complex activities from labour-exchange to house moving to wedding preparations, to feasts are co-ordinated by networks of understanding and practice. It is the same with boycotts, wage 'negotiations', the refusal of tenants to compete with one another, or the conspiracy of silence surrounding thefts. No formal organisations are created because none are required; and yet a form of co-ordination is achieved which alerts us that what is happening is not just individual action.

In light of these considerations, then, let us return briefly to the question of intention. For many forms of peasant resistance, we have every reason to expect that the actors will remain *mute* about their intentions. Their safety may depend on silence and anonymity; the kind of resistance itself may depend for its effectiveness on the *appearance* of conformity; their intentions may be so embedded in the peasant subculture *and* in the routine, taken-for-granted struggle to provide for the subsistence and survival of the household so to remain inarticulate. The fish do not talk about the water.

In one sense, of course, their intentions are inscribed in the acts themselves. A peasant soldier who, like others, deserts the army is, in effect, saying by his act that the purposes of this institution and the risks and hardships it entails will not prevail over his family or personal needs. To put it another way, the state and its army has failed sufficiently to commit this particular subject to its enterprise so as to retain his compliance. A harvest labourer who steals paddy from his employer is 'saying' that his need for rice takes precedence over the formal property rights of his boss.

When it comes to those social settings where the *material interests* of appropriating classes are directly in conflict with the peasantry (rents, wages, employment, taxes, conscription, the division of the harvest) we can, I think, infer something of intentions from the nature of the actions themselves. This is especially the case when there is a systematic pattern of actions which mitigate or deny a claim on their surplus. Evidence about intentions is, of course, always welcome but we should not expect too much. For this reason, the definition of resistance given earlier places particular emphasis on the effort to thwart material and symbolic claims from dominant classes. The goal, after all, of the great bulk of peasant resistance is not directly to overthrow or transform a system of domination but rather to survive – today, this week, this season – within it. The usual goal of peasants, as Hobsbawm has so aptly put it, is *'working the system to their minimum disadvantage'* [1973: 12]. Their persistent attempts to 'nibble away' may backfire, they may marginally alleviate exploitation, they may amount to a renegotiation of the limits of appropriation, they may change the course of subsequent development, and they may more rarely help bring the system down. These, however, are possible consequences. Their intention, by contrast, is nearly always survival and persistence. The pursuit of that end may require, depending on circumstances, either the petty resistance we have seen or more dramatic actions of self-defence. In any event, most of their efforts will be seen by appropriating classes as truculence, deceit, shirking, pilfering, arrogance – in short, all the labels devised to denigrate the many faces of resistance. The definition of appropriating classes may, at other times, transform what amounts to nothing more than the unreflective struggle for subsistence into an act of defiance.

It should be apparent that resistance is not simply whatever peasants do to maintain themselves and their households. Much of what they do is to be understood as compliance, however grudging. Survival as petty commodity producers or labourers may impel some to save themselves at the expense of their fellows. The poor landless labourer who steals paddy from another poor man or who outbids him for a tenancy is surviving but he is surely not resisting in the sense defined here. One of the key questions that must be asked about any system of domination is the extent to which it succeeds in reducing subordinate classes to purely 'beggar thy neighbour' strategies for survival. Certain combinations of atomisation, terror, repression, and pressing material needs can indeed achieve the ultimate dream of domination: to have the dominated exploit each other.

Allowing that only those survival strategies which deny or mitigate claims from appropriating classes can be called resistance, we are nevertheless left with a vast range of actions to consider. Their variety conceals a basic continuity. That continuity lies in the history of the persistent efforts of relatively autonomous petty commodity producers to defend their fundamental material and physical interests and to reproduce themselves. At different times and places they have defended themselves against the corvée, taxes, and conscription of the traditional agrarian state, against the colonial state, against the inroads of capitalism (for example, rents, interest, proletarianisation, mechanisation), against the modern capitalist state and, it should be added, against many purportedly socialist states as well. The revolution, when and if it does come, may eliminate many of the worst evils of the ancien régime, but it is rarely if ever the end of peasant resistance. For the radical elites who capture the state are likely to have different goals in mind than their erstwhile peasant supporters. They may envisage a col- lectivised agriculture while the peasantry clings to its smallholdings; they may want a centralised political structure while the peasantry is wedded to local autonomy; they may want to tax the countryside in order to indus- trialise; and they will almost certainly wish to strengthen the state *vis-à-vis* civil society. It therefore becomes possible for an astute observer like Goran Hyden to find remarkable parallels between the earlier resistance of the Tanzanian peasantry to colonialism and capitalism and its *current* resistance to the institutions and policies of the *socialist* state of Tanzania today [*Hyden*, 1980: *passim*]. He provides a gripping account of how the 'peasant mode of production' – by footdragging, by privatising work and land that have been appropriated by the state, by evasion, by flight, and by 'raiding' government programs for its own purposes – has thwarted the plans of the state. In Vietnam, also, after the revolution was consummated in the south as well as in the north, everyday forms of peasant resistance have continued. The surreptitious expansion of private plots, the withdrawal of labour from state enterprises for household production, the failure to deliver grain and livestock to the state, the 'appropriation' of state credits and resources by households and work teams, and the steady growth of the black market, attest to the tenacity of petty commodity production under socialist state forms.[27] The stubborn, persistent, and irreducible forms of resistance we have been examining may thus represent the truly durable weapons of the weak both before and *after* the revolution.

NOTES

1. See, for example, Barrington Moore, Jr., *The Social Basis of Dictatorship and Democracy* (Boston: Boston Press, 1966); Jeffrey M. Paige, *Agrarian Revolution: Social Movements and Export Agriculture in the Underdeveloped World* (New York: Free Press, 1975); Eric R. Wolf, *Peasant Wars of the Twentieth Century* (New Haven: Yale University Press, 1976); Samuel L. Popkin, *The Rational Peasant* (Berkeley: University of California Press, 1969).
2. For an example of such temporary gains, see the fine study by E.J. Hobsbawm and George Rudé, *Captain Swing* (New York: Pantheon Books, 1968), pp. 281–99.
3. Some of these issues are examined in Scott, 'Revolution in the Revolution: Peasants and Commisars', *Theory and Society*, Vol. 7, Nos. 1, 2 (1979), pp. 97–134.

4. See the account and analysis by Michael Adas, 'From Avoidance to Confrontation: Peasant Protest in Precolonial and Colonial Southeast Asia', *Comparative Studies in Society and History*, Vol. 23, No. 2 (April 1981), pp. 217–47.

5. R.C. Cobb, *The Police and the People: French Popular Protest, 1789–1820* (Oxford: Clarendon Press, 1970), pp. 96–7. For a gripping account of self-mutilation to avoid conscription, see Emile Zola, *La Terre*, translated by Douglas Parmee (Harmondsworth: Penguin, 1980).

6. For a fascinating account of such resistance in Tanzania, see Goran Hyden, *Beyond Ujamaa in Tanzania* (London: Heinneman, 1980). For the consequences of short-sighted agrarian policy imposed from above see Robert Bates, *Markets and States in Tropical Africa: The Political Basis of Agricultural Policies* (Berkeley: University of California Press, 1981).

7. The best, most complete account of this may be found in Lim Teck Ghee, *Peasants and their Agricultural Economy in Colonial Malaya, 1874–1941* (Kuala Lumpur: Oxford University Press, 1977). See also the persuasive argument in Donald M. Nonini, Paul Diener, and Eugene E. Robkin, 'Ecology and Evolution: Population, Primitive Accumulation, and the Malay Peasantry', unpublished ms., 1979.

8. A classic example is the Soviet collectivisation campaign in which the widespread opposition to joining the Kolkhoz was never widely publicised until given official warrant by Stalin in his 'Dizzy with Success' Speech in March 1930. Before this, one would never have imagined that coercion had been used (the euphemism for coercion was 'bureaucratic ordering-about'), that an enormous depletion of livestock had taken place in response to the campaign, or that the opposition to collectivisation was as strong among middle peasants as among the kulaks. See R.W. Davies, *The Socialist Offensive: The Collectivisation of Soviet Agriculture, 1928–1930* (London: Macmillan, 1980), Chs. 6, 7.

9. But not entirely. District level records are likely to prove rewarding in this respect as district officials attempt to explain the shortfall in, say, tax receipts or conscription figures to their superiors in the capital. One imagines also that the informal, oral record is abundant – for example, informal cabinet or ministerial meetings called to deal with policy failures caused by rural insubordination.

10. The partial exception is, of course, anthropology.

11. I by no means wish to suggest that violence born of revenge, hatred, and fury play no role – only that they do not exhaust the subject as Zola and others imply. It is certainly true as Cobb (op. cit., pp. 89–90) claims, that George Rudé (*The Crowd in History, 1730–1848* (New York: Wiley and Sons, 1964)) has gone too far in turning rioters into sober, domesticated bourgeois political actors.

12. For an extended account see James C. Scott, *Everyday Forms of Peasant Resistance* (New Haven: Yale University Press, forthcoming), Chs. 3, 4.

13. It is worth noting that neither outright repression nor the duress of the quotidian would be as effective in limiting options if the peasantry of the Muda Plain had their backs truly against the wall. Thanks to the booming urban sector in Malaysia a fair number of those most disadvantaged by double-cropping can exercise the historic response of peasants to oppression: flight. Were these alternatives closed off, the same level of repression would undoubtedly be less effective.

14. Rosni, a widow, is renowned for her hard work and independence while Rokiah's husband is considered rather weak-minded, so that Rokiah is normally seen as the head of her household, making all the basic decisions. Such women, especially if they are past child-bearing age, are treated virtually as 'honorary males' and are exempt from many of the customary requirements of modesty and deference expected of women in Malay society.

15. The literal translation of the Malay saying is 'Angry with his rice, he throws it out the window – giving it to the chickens to eat' (*Marah sama nasi, tauk, bagi ayam makan*).

16. The localism of the boycott and the absence of institutions that might have enforced it throughout the regional labour market were devastating handicaps as they are so often in peasant politics. Thus women from Sedaka, while boycotting some local farmers, were

accepting work *elsewhere* thereby occasionally serving unwittingly as 'strike-breakers' in other Muda villages. And, of course, women from these villages, or others like them, were hired to help break the boycott in Sedaka. It was a classic example of the crippling effects of solidarity when it is only local.

17. For an examination of other forms of routine resistance including other kinds of theft, see my *Everyday Class Relations* (New Haven: Yale Press, forthcoming), Ch. 7.

18. This figure is a *crude* estimate. Such paddy is stolen by prying apart the boards of the granary or by making a hole through which paddy can be collected. Although many farmers mark the level of paddy inside the *jelapang* periodically, it is difficult to know precisely how much has been taken. As a rule, only well-off farmers have such rice barns; the poor keep their paddy in a corner of the house.

19. There is, however, a more subtle means of 'naming' the suspect which amounts to a traditional form of 'letting it be known' (*cara sembunyi tau*). This consists of consulting one of the medicine men (*bomoh*) in the district who have acquired a reputation for finding lost property or identifying the thief. After learning the particulars, the *bomoh* will use incantations (*jampi*) and conjure up the form of the thief in water prepared especially for the occasion. Not surprisingly, the visage thus called forth, typically is seen to be that of the man whom the client had all along suspected. In the case of stolen paddy, the purpose is not so much to recover the paddy as to identify the thief. The farmer, when he returns to the village, will tell his friends that the *bomoh* saw someone who looked like so-and-so. The news will spread and the suspected thief will learn that he is being watched without a direct accusation, let alone a police report, ever having been made. Thus Haji Kadir said that the *bomoh* had, in his case, seen Taib and another unidentified man in the water. If, indeed, Taib was the culprit, Haji Kadir hoped that this roundabout accusation would prevent any subsequent thefts from that quarter. On at least two occasions, however, villagers recall that some or all of the paddy taken has mysteriously reappeared after consulting a *bomoh*. The kind of circumspection employed by those few farmers who actually resort to the *bomoh* is another indication that an open confrontation is considered dangerous.

20. For some interesting parallels, see E.P. Thompson, 'The Crime of Anonymity' in Douglas Hay, *et al., Albion's Fatal Tree*, pp. 255–344.

21. See E.J. Hobsbawm's *Primitive Rebels: Studies in Archaic Forms of Social Movement in the 19th and 20th Centuries* (New York: Norton, 1965). Hobsbawm's otherwise illuminating account is, I believe, burdened unduly with a unilinear theory of lower class history which anticipates that every primitive form of resistance will, in due course, be superceded by a more progressive form until a mature Marxist-Leninist vision is reached.

22. See James C. Scott, *Everyday Forms of Peasant Resistance* (New Haven: Yale University Press, 1984), Ch. 8.

23. See Allan Wildman, 'The February Revolution in the Russian Army', *Soviet Studies*, Vol. 22, No. 1 (July 1970), pp. 3–23; Marc Ferro, 'The Russian Soldier in 1917: Undisciplined, Patriotic, and Revolutionary,' *Slavic Review*, Vol. 30, No. 3 (Sept. 1971), pp. 483–512; Barrington Moore, *Injustice* (White Plains, New York: M.E. Sharpe, 1978), p. 364, and Theda Skopol, *States and Social Revolutions* (Cambridge: Cambridge University Press, 1979), pp. 135–8. There is a consensus that Bolshevik propaganda at the front was *not* instrumental in provoking these desertions.

24. One may wish to call the land seizures and sacking of gentry property a revolutionary act, and it was certainly revolutionary in its consequences in 1917. But it was a largely spontaneous affair out of the control of any party and it is extremely unlikely that those seizing the land self-consciously saw themselves as bringing about a revolutionary government, let alone a Bolshevik one. See Skocpol, op.cit., pp. 135, 138.

25. The initial successes of Solidarity in Poland can in a similar fashion be attributed largely to the fact that the unpopular regime could not count on its own army to actively suppress the rebellious civilian population and was instead forced to rely on the hated paramilitary police, the 'Zomos'.

26. Such resistance is not, of course, the monopoly of lower classes. Tax evasion and the so-

called 'black' economy in advance capitalist countries are *also* forms of resistance, albeit pursued with most vigour and success by middle and upper classes.
27. See, for example, the article in this volume by Christine White.

REFERENCES

Adas, Michael, 1981, 'From Avoidance to Confrontation: Peasant Protest in Precolonial and Colonial Southeast Asia', *Comparative Studies in Society and History*, Vol. 23, No. 2, April, pp. 217–47.
Bates, Robert, 1981, *Markets and States in Tropical Africa: The Political Basis of Agricultural Policies*, Berkeley: University of California Press.
Carr, E. H., 1966, *The Bolshevik Revolution: 1917–1923*, Vol. 1, Harmondsworth: Penguin.
Cobb, R.C., 1970, *The Police and the People: French Popular Protest, 1789–1820*, Oxford: Clarendon Press.
Davies, R.W., 1980, *The Socialist Offensive: The Collectivisation of Soviet Agriculture, 1928–1930*, London: Macmillan.
Ferro, Marc, 1971, 'The Russian Soldier in 1917: Undisciplined, Patriotic, and Revolutionary', *Slavic Review*, Vol. 30, No. 3, Sept.
Genovese, Eugene, 1974, *Roll, Jordan Roll*, New York: Pantheon Books, 1974.
Ghee, Lim Teck, 1977, *Peasants and their Agricultural Economy in Colonial Malaya, 1874–1941*, Kuala Lumpur: Oxford University Press.
Hobsbawm, Eric J. and George Rudé, 1968, *Captain Swing*, New York: Pantheon Books.
Hobsbawm, Eric J., 1965, *Primitive Rebels: Studies in Archaic Forms of Social Movement in the 19th and 20th Centuries*, New York: Norton.
Hobsbawm, Eric J., 1973, 'Peasants and Politics', *Journal of Peasant Studies*, Vol. 1, No. 1.
Hyden, Goran, 1980, *Beyond Ujamaa in Tanzania*, London: Heinemann.
Lewis, Oscar, 1964, *Pedro Martinez: A Mexican Peasant and his Family*, New York: Vintage Books.
Marx, Karl, 1970, *Capital*, Vol. 1, London.
Moore, Barrington, Jr., 1966, *The Social Basis of Dictatorship and Democracy*, Boston: Beacon Press.
Moore, Barrington, 1978, *Injustice*, White Plains, New York: M.E. Sharpe.
Mullin, Gerald, 1972, *Flight and Rebellion*, New York: Oxford University Press.
Nonini, Donald M., Paul Diener and Eugene E. Robkin, 1979, 'Ecology and Evolution: Population, Primitive Accumulation, and the Malay Peasantry', unpublished ms.
Paige, Jeffrey M., 1975, *Agrarian Revolution: Social Movements and Export Agriculture in the Underdeveloped World*, New York: Free Press.
Patnaik, Utsa, 1979, 'Neo-populism and Marxism: The Chayanovian View of the Agrarian Question and its Fundamental Fallacy,' *Journal of Peasant Studies*, Vol. 6, No. 4, July.
Popkin, Samuel L., 1969, *The Rational Peasant*, Berkeley: University of California Press.
Rudé, George, 1964, *The Crowd in History, 1730–1848*, New York: Wiley and Sons.
Scott, James C., 1976, *The Moral Economy of the Peasant*, New Haven: Yale University Press.
Scott, James C., 1979, 'Revolution in the Revolution: Peasants and Commisars', *Theory and Society*, Vol. 7, No. 1.
Scott, James C., 1984, *Everyday Forms of Peasant Resistance*, New Haven: Yale University Press.
Skocpol, Theda, 1979, *States and Social Revolutions*, Cambridge: Cambridge University Press.
Thompson, E.P., 'The Crime of Anonymity' in Douglas Hay *et al.*, *Albion's Fatal Tree*.

Thompson, E.P., 'Eighteenth-Century English Society: Class Struggle Without Class?', *Social History*, Vol. 398–399.

Wildman, Allan, 1970, 'The February Revolution in the Russian Army', *Soviet Studies*, Vol. 22, No. 1, July.

Wolf, Eric R., 1969, *Peasant Wars of the Twentieth Century*, New York: Harper and Row.

Zola, Emile, 1980, *La Terre*, translated by Douglas Parmée, Harmondsworth: Penguin.

Patrolling the Middle-Ground: Methodological Perspectives on 'Everyday Peasant Resistance'

Andrew Turton*

In the Introduction to this volume James Scott speaks of 'everyday resistance' as 'a vast and relatively unexplored middle-ground of peasant politics between passivity and open, collective defiance'. Here I wish rather to conceptualise a middle-ground in-between everyday and exceptional forms of resistance, a middle-ground, a terrain of struggle, on which practices may possibly serve to link the other two terms; although such linkages are not assured. For I also have reservations as to the appropriateness of 'passivity' as a way of referring to apparent non-resistance or acquiescence in what some others, or the same peasants at other times, are 'resisting'. The notion of passivity seems to reintroduce the image of 'supine victims'. As Gordon puts it in his commentary on Foucault's discussions of power, strategy and resistance – which have been among several perspectives orienting this study:

> The existence of those who seem not to rebel is a warren of minute, individual, autonomous tactics and strategies which counter and inflect the visible facts of overall domination, and whose purposes and calculations, desires and choices resist any simple division into the political and the apolitical [*Foucault*, 1980: 251].

What follows here are some critical reflections of a methodological nature which have arisen in a specific context of research into the recent experiences of poor farmers in Thailand in their efforts to organise themselves defensively and more assertively on issues of livelihood and social power.** These experiences include a more mobile and widespread, almost national, peasant movement in 1974–75 (see Kanjana [1984] and Kanoksak [1984]),

*Department of Anthropology and Sociology, School of Oriental and African Studies, University of London, Malet Street, London WC1E 7HP.

**The research project 'Popular Participation in Rural Thailand' was sponsored by the United Nations Research Institute for Social Development and funded by the Norwegian government. The research team included members of poor farmers' organisations, development workers from several non-governmental organisations, and academic social science researchers from Chulalongkorn University Social Research Institute, the Thai Khadi Research Institute of Thammasat University, and the Faculty of Social Sciences, Chiangmai University. The author is heavily indebted to the collective work of all participants, but here bears sole responsibility for any inaccuracy or misjudgement.

its defeat and disbandment, and subsequent smaller-scale, more localised efforts. The aim here is to open up some perspectives, not to attempt a comprehensive theoretical approach or to provide detailed documentation. There is also a deliberate foregrounding of political and ideological dimensions, a selective emphasis on the analysis of the exercise of power which is intended to be complementary to a more strictly economic analysis. For it is not only 'claims on its surplus' that are being resisted by peasants, but also other claims and assaults on their social being in a wider sense including cultural forms of life, their dignity and 'human' value in its specific cultural conceptions. 'Everyday forms of resistance' are thus to a large extent responses to 'everyday forms of oppression or domination', and these, too, need to be examined. I start with some rather general reflections, in a deconstructive spirit, on the two principal terms of the debate in this volume: 'peasant' and 'resistance'; and then develop themes more specifically with reference to research in Thailand.

Since we must be talking about particular rural producers in particular locations within societies at particular historical times, we are obliged to specify those societies and conjunctures. At least we should specify state, power bloc, the politically, economically and culturally dominant classes, and the productive and social relations of those rural producers. It matters particularly whether we are dealing with rural producers under a dominant form of capitalism, which I judge to be the case in a number of South-east Asian countries, albeit in historically and locally specific forms. For if this is the case, the 'peasant' problem diminishes relatively in significance and a new class problematic emerges in which the 'peasantry', or substantial sections of it and while remaining distinct, are part of a new working class in the making. Despite the apparent so-called 'non-disappearance' of the peasant, it seems to me sometimes now that much of what has been written of peasants in previous epochs – for example, using such concepts as millenarianism, moral economy, images of limited good [*sic*], etc. – belongs to the prehistory of the rural producers of the late twentieth century. There is also a danger that by insistence on a Peasant Subject, social movements which involve more than just peasants are left on one side, which they cannot be for long; nor is it only in specific social movements that peasants may be allied with others.

Even when such global questions have been addressed, most of the difficulties remain. Which members (by gender, age, ethnic and cultural criteria, etc.) of which rural classes, strata and fractions are acting, and in what combinations? How collectively and autonomously are they acting, and with what leadership, encouragement or support, if any? This already anticipates the problematic distinction between rare, collective rebellions and everyday, uncoordinated individual struggles, which I shall discuss later. For not until we can specify who are the subjects of this activity, and in what relations of production and political structures they find themselves, can we be in a position to ask what they are resisting.

Even then we can first ask, while trying to avoid such pitfalls as nominalism, ethnocentrism, ahistoricism, etc., how we and others use concepts of resistance. For a start we might note a two-dimensionality in the term: both *successfully* to oppose, perhaps stopping short of overcoming, and to *attempt* to oppose, with varying degrees of success. We can speak of a range of strength, of degrees proof [*sic*] against, of degrees of impedance from, say, a momentary, scarcely uttered verbal refusal, to a prolonged, materially sustained immunity. 'Resistance', as a concept, shares with related concepts (insubordination, protest, opposition, struggle, rebellion, revolution ...) a basic meaning of *negation*. Like them it refers, in a fluid way, to forms of social action which vary as to physical strength, critical awareness, effectiveness, collectivity, social range, etc. capable of being judged either more 'conservative' or 'progressive'. We must also note that 'resistance' is not a monopoly of the subordinate and exploited: bureaucratic footdragging is but one common example. An original sense of impede was the non-metaphorical shackling of the feet of, subordinate, others.

While it is not possible here to document in detail the Thai language of resistance in use, we may note a variety of words which, often in characteristic combination – doubled and quadrupled, for example, *totaan khatkhwang* – seem to express a range of meanings comparable to those we are using in English here. They range from the actions of armies and resistance movements to face-to-face disagreement and petty acts of covert obstruction. For summary purposes I shall resort to the not entirely satisfactory exposition of some dictionary entries for these commonest of Thai terms:

to – stand against, fight, contend, resist;
which is used in many doublets, notably with:

taan – stop, resist, oppose, strive against, withstand, counter.

khat – block, choke, clog, hinder, obstruct; stop, prevent, resist, retard, oppose, deny, interfere, object, refuse, disagree, conflict;
which is also used in many doublets, notably with:

khwang – lie athwart, get in the way, restrain, hinder, prevent, oppose.

What is being resisted (and what combination of things), and what is not being resisted, and why? Rural producers do indeed resist daily, above all, 'natural' forces, and this no doubt helps to shape the forms of social and political resistance. What is being resisted immediately in any particular case is, I suppose, the perceived, experienced effects – whether more or less physical, for example, hunger or insult or some combination – of a perceived or experienced relationship: other people or agencies variously held responsible for the effects. The actual experience may be of, or rather be expressed in terms of: economic exploitation, infliction of pain and suffering, coercion, bullying, intimidation, indignity, intolerance, bigotry, corruption, immorality, injustice etc. We need to attend particularly to the cultural idioms in which these experiences are expressed and the contexts of their use.

Individuals or sets of individuals, multifariously constituted social subjects, will have various sources of advice as to who or what are the causes of these ill effects. They are not likely to need help in being discontented with the ill effects in the first place, or to move to the initial refusal. As William Cobbett said, the rural rioters in England in the 1830s had plenty of reason to riot without him: 'Why need the parsons hunt about after *lecturers* as the cause of the discontents?' (cited in Hobsbawm and Rudé [1973: 47] original italics). It may be that to a degree people accept that they are suffering from something they are not, with negative experience and the authorship elided as in a medical image: 'you are suffering [from] a disease', for example, 'the problem is poverty'. In the case of Thailand, instances might be those peasants in the communist camp who were encouraged, in the early 1970s at least, to fight 'revisionism'; or those in the government camp who are told that the greatest current threat to their well-being is 'communism'. The causes of the suffering, the responsible and determining agencies and relationships *may* thus be unclear to the actor in every degree and, therefore, the target of eventual resistance be misplaced. The people, the social relationships – more or less or not at all appropriately identified – which are actually resisted may be, for example: landlords, merchants, moneylenders, managers of subsidiaries of transnational corporations, state and other officials, religious figures, men ... or they may be bandits, insurgents, criminals, ill-intentioned neighbours, middlemen, ethnic minorities, foreigners, etc. Or opposition may be directed towards the self (own bad nature, immorality, *karma*, etc.) or towards 'superhuman' or 'supernatural' agencies.

I have said that in order to speak of 'resistance', or anything similar, we must first attempt to specify the social relationships which support, constrain, threaten or exploit the resister. To do this adequately we need to give an account of structures and processes of power, and not just institutional forms, but also its exercise in manifold local and informal situations and milieux, what Foucault calls its 'capillary' forms, 'polymorphous techniques of subjugation', the 'micro-physics of power'. At the same time we should relate these to specific concentrations of power, whether formally institutionalised or not, to state, power bloc, dominant groups, etc. In other words there can be no adequate study of forms of resistance without a prior and simultaneous study of forms of domination – forms of disqualification, subordination, penetration, menace, suppression, attack; and also co-optation, toleration, temptation, donation, etc. – by controlling groups and classes and their agencies. This should illuminate not only what is being or might be resisted, but also the constraining powers which limit, and occasionally enable, forms and strategies of resistance themselves. A particular emphasis which I would give is that the examination of power should include the techniques and modalities of both more physically coercive forms of domination and more ideological or discursive forms, *and* the relations between the two, relations in which, to anticipate, fear may be a crucial factor. For the better we are able to conceptualise the limits – the extent, extremities and limitations – of domination, the better we can identify and assess past achievements and present potentialities of popular struggles and acts of resistance, and the better we can address ourselves to the problem of what Raymond Williams has called 'emergent cultural practice' or the emergence – and submerged persistence – of what Wertheim has called 'contrapuntal value systems'. In this way too we may avoid mere documentation of more or less obvious, phenomenal instances of forms of resistance, of how peasants resist.

I have elsewhere attempted to characterise the heterogeneous class nature of the contemporary Thai state, and the multiple alliances and configurations of forces which constitute a ruling 'power bloc', in which a capitalist bourgeoisie is not the predominant element. While the state does indeed partly serve the interests of a capitalist class, it also has a momentum of its own and its own somewhat hybrid, parasitic and predatory interests. This suggested a specific kind of relative autonomy of the state, and disjunction between economic and political-ideological domination. This I argued was particularly relevant for the analysis of local powers in the countryside, themselves of heterogeneous class composition, which to some extent combine with or are manifestations of state powers or may correspond to competing factions within state apparatuses [*Turton*, 1985].

This opened up a perspective on 'local powers', power blocs and coalitions which were seen as an important mediation and localisation of the contradiction between state and capitalist spheres on the one hand and the majority of rural producers on the other. At the local level we find a complex overlapping and interpenetration of economic, political, administrative and cultural agencies, relations and interests, and a characteristic combination of formal and informal, official and non-official, public and private, legal and illegal activities. While not best viewed in terms of structures, institutions or state apparatuses, they do have their 'vertical' and 'horizontal' linkages and forms of consolidation. Examples were given, and they can be multiplied, of cross-cutting and mutually supporting involvement of powerful figures in and through local administrative structures, paramilitary organisations, 'mafia' style economic activity, crime, corruption, etc. These powers constituted a crucial means, direct and indirect, intended and unintended, and through a range of normative and remunerative sanctions, backed by coercion, by which the state is able to prevent, mitigate and suppress the expression of conflict between rural classes, and in a sense the very formation of those classes.

In so far as this nexus can be established it allows for a conceptualisation of sites and spaces of struggle to secure and challenge hegemony, of the conditions of any form of resistance. If this nexus has any conceptual validity, then one might say that the dominant contradiction is between 'the people' and 'the power bloc'. It might then be said to follow that any local 'peasant' resistance – whether or not consciously political – against members of the 'power bloc' *and*, or *through*, its local agents and allies, policies and projects – have an added political significance and may be relevant to the struggles of others than peasants, other sectors of the rural and non-rural population. One set of instances by way of illustration is the tactical challenges to established local powers constituted by various small-scale organisations of poor farmers acting through various forms of calculated involvement and non-involvement in farmers' associations and sub-district councils.

Thus the finer our recognition and appreciation of agencies and instruments of domination the better we may be able to assess whether they are being resisted, or in what ways are perceived to be capable of being resisted or not; and the better we may recognise certain actions *as being* forms of resistance. As an illustrative example, to the extent that schools and schooling are seen as in part the instruments of the powers of the state and dominant sectors of society, then such phenomena as truancy, popular criticisms of teachers, official co-option of teachers into paramilitary type organisations, local attempts at self-education, or even demands for more and more appropriate education, may take on a new and more political significance.

The modalities of domination are no respecters of institutional boundaries, and even the more official forms are pervasive and permeate many areas of daily life. Drawing from and adding to instances suggested by Foucault, we need to identify a range of constraints and forms of social discipline: training, examinations, punishments; regulations, registrations and licensing; supervision and surveillance; the political *techniques du corps*, the proxemics and kinesics of domination. This military-bureaucratic imagery is particularly appropriate for the Thai social formation and contrasts with village-community and family values. The methodological point is that any, even barely conscious, acts which tend to negate or counter deeply engrained bureaucratic mentalities and forms of discipline may be highly significant. Thus, to take a seemingly trivial instance, avoiding or neglecting registration for various purposes or carrying identity cards (a frequent petty offence) may be practically unwise, but it is at the least symptomatic: in 1975, during a more open political period, some villagers in central Thailand did actually turn in or burn their identity cards as part of protests.

From a theoretical or methodological point of view the *form* of resistance as such is of less interest than an analysis of a particular social relation and its context in which the form arises. The dynamics of relationship and context must be theoretically elaborated, and one aspect, selectively emphasised here, is the modalities of ideological domination. Concepts of ideology can be usefully developed via concepts of discourse, which allow for the conceptualisation of procedures for the authorisation, disqualification and restriction of discourse, of discursive practices and their material or physical adjuncts. I have elsewhere elaborated on such concepts of 'restriction of discourse', of rules of – or if not rules, then perhaps inexplicit means resulting in – obedience and obeisance, terms which have, as in some popular Thai equivalents, a root meaning of listening to, and so of receiving orders and instructions [*Turton*, 1984]. Thus the ideological inculcation of knowledge of and respect for the social division of labour in the widest sense directs the social subject to know her/his place in it, and when, where, how, of what, and to whom to speak. It establishes an authoritative – and it may be judged authoritarian – context of speaking and social communication, of discourse in the fullest sense of what constitutes legitimate and prevailing forms of knowledge and expression. Once again the methodological advantage gained from such a perspective is that we can see various 'disobedient' tactics and behaviours in a rather new light or see them for the first time *as* disobedient; for example, forms of dissimulation, false deference, feigned ignorance, and secrecy on the part of subordinates. We may attribute a new significance to instances of speaking up and speaking out, or of parallel *sotto voce* commentaries perhaps in another dialect or language, or of forms of dialogue and meetings which selectively exclude dominant others. These might be said to be examples of 'restrictive practices' in reverse. Of similar import may be the reproduction, or reconstruction, and dissemination of officially excluded or downgraded forms of discourse and knowledge, of inherited popular cultural practices – which might, for example, be alternative and local religious, medical, linguistic, musical or other practices – or the selective creation or appropriation of new elements from other areas of society – forms of association, popular musical culture, etc.

A theoretical concern with connections between more and less physical means of coercion, between physically violent and ideological techniques of domination, between force and consensual norms, and a better theoretical understanding of the inadequacy of these dichotomies, should help us to conceptualise and evaluate the dialectics of resistance. Mental and physical, 'hard' and 'soft' techniques are not so distinct in practice either. Much of the ordinary language of cognition and learning is very concrete and physical – there is a large range of terms such as 'getting hold of an idea', 'driving a point home', etc. – even the more abstract sounding 'inculcation' used earlier (making a strong impression, forceful teaching) has a root meaning of stamping with the heel (from the Latin *calx*) and meets with resistance in 'recalcitrance' which shares the same anatomical root. Footdragging, digging the feet in, or 'voting with their feet' through flight, etc. are conscious acts of the downtrodden. Apparently discursive 'interpellations' of human beings as social subjects (recruiting, addressing, labelling – including self-addressed labels) are backed by, or intimately accompanied by, non-discursive sanctions. The now classic case of the *gendarme* 'hailing' the suspect is quickly followed by the snapping on of handcuffs: any concept of emancipation must mean the loosening of both material and 'mind-forged manacles'. One way to go beyond these dichotomies is to examine 'the necessary ideological mediation of force or sanctions', a mediation which

Therborn suggests operates through fear: 'force and violence operate as a form of rule only through the ideological mechanism of fear' [*Therborn*, 1980: 98].

I was drawn to consider these issues when trying to think about a pervasive phenomenon in the Thai countryside – and no doubt found widely elsewhere in some form or another – namely, the labelling and accusation of subjects as 'communist'. This is particularly relevant to the concerns of the present collection because it is, above all, a weapon against the non-insurgent, although not perhaps the exclusively 'everyday' 'resister'. It does, however, occur in a context where there is an avowedly communist insurgency which involves some peasants in its movement, currently at a very low level. Such labelling has the effect, to some extent intentionally, of 'excommunicating' the subject, and even objectifying to the extent that the accusation may justify and license the killing (however illegal) of anyone previously (or even *post mortem*) labelled 'communist'. Almost any independent rural initiative outside official definitions runs the risk of attracting the charge of being 'communist' from some quarter or other. This phenomenon of accusation can only be understood in a multi-determined context of ideological and forceful domination. Some empirical elements of this context can be summarily adduced. They include: increased police and military activity and presence in the countryside; the co-option by the state of local 'intellectuals' (junior officials, teachers, village appointees and committee members, etc.) as paramilitary trainers, leaders and informers of various sorts; the nature of local powers discussed earlier which have access to the coercive apparatus of the state as well as more autonomous means. These factors have some bearing on a very high rural homicide rate where many instances (some revenge killings, police 'death squads', 'extra-judicial' killings of various kinds, etc.) can be shown to be of a political nature. Also to be taken into account are previously existing popular mentalities of fear, and years of groundwork – institutional, legal, ideological, etc. – preparing for a negative reflex to the word 'communist' and its associations. So that while the scale of violence is perhaps measurably less than in, say, some Central American countries or elsewhere, the *threat* of death is made real and immediate; there is a 'climate of fear'; assent to dominant discourse is increasingly 'demanded with menaces'; the lure is baited.

Another crucial mediation between the ideological message and the ultimate sanction is *surveillance*, a practical procedure which has been raised to conceptual status by Giddens [1981] and by Foucault in his discussion of social discipline. Dominant discourse does not only say 'Now hear this!' but also 'You are being watched!'. Relatively low-intensity surveillance is not new, but more organised forms seem to be on the increase with a variety of categories of spies and informers and of their training, functions and rewards. Philip Hirsch has discussed the way in which resettlement villages are physically organised with roads and grid pattern layout of houses officially for 'ease of administration' and to enable village officials to 'watch over everyone', and of villagers' resistance to this by among other things preferring to live in field houses away from the village [*Hirsch*, 1985: 13–14; 28–9].

Once again these methodological considerations can help us to recognise constraints on resistance and to recognise as such and evaluate forms of resistance to these and other forms of control in spite of this fairly systematic intimidation and surveillance. For instance, in such situations fear is obviously a proper response, a human response, in some degree. How that response is modulated in practice and in discourse is another matter: for fear is not necessarily timidity. Nor is respect necessarily deference (or vice versa if you like); nor are Schweikian kinds of 'non-bravery' necessarily cowardice. A qualified or critical acquiescence in imposed roles and identities can be discerned in numerous small-scale acts of defiance. For example, the paradoxical *acceptance* (even if only humourously or in private) of the label 'communist'; the reported enthusiastic shouting, at the end of a 'Village Scout' ceremony abjuring the enemies of nation, religion and monarch, not of '*komunit*' (communist) as in the official liturgy, but the nicely rhyming '*tucarit*' (dishonest ones); or 'Village Defence Volunteers' *insisting* on having discussions about 'national security' and attempting to define real dangers, both local and national, and in ways which challenge state agencies and policies.

I suggested at the outset that we might look again at the distinction between, on the one hand, rarer peasant uprisings and 'open collective defiance' and, on the other hand, more common, indeed everyday forms of peasant resistance which are less confrontational, more individualistic acts requiring little or no co-ordination. Indeed something of what I had in mind had been anticipated in James Scott's Introduction when he says that routine forms of resistance 'are generally underwritten by a sub-culture of resistance' and that they 'may, cumulatively, have an appreciable impact on class and authority relations in the countryside'. This already allows for the possibility of a greater degree of collective, conscious action and a wider and longer-term effectiveness than some uses of the notion 'everyday resistance' might suggest.

The rarer uprisings have recently been the focus of scholarly attention in Thailand (see especially Chatthip [1984]; Tanabe [1984]). They have historically nearly all been regional in range, and some have been relatively small-scale, if larger and more important than official records allow. There are also many instances, few of them documented in academic literature, of rather heroic acts undertaken by individuals, usually in defiance of some local authority and of a quite confrontational kind. They can be seen as champions of at least locally generalisable causes of suffering and injustice and are likely to have a degree of at least tacit local support. When in the past such individuals have established local support then they may merge as a type with the smaller-scale uprisings referred to earlier. Individual stands of this kind are sometimes remembered as part of the prehistory of later local struggles. Finally, many acts can quite readily be thought of as everyday and more individualistic resistance: from year in, year out, defiance of laws restricting subsistence economic activity (hunting, gathering and other use of forest reserve land; unlicensed slaughter of animals for meat, brewing and distilling, etc.) to regular joking and cursing about higher powers and authorities.

It might also be useful, if only heuristically, to conceptualise another category of 'in-between' forms of resistance: 'in-between' in terms of time, scale and space, and of mediation. However, it is not really a question of mutually exclusive conceptual categories, nor of phenomena clearly distinguishable on an empirical basis. The aim here is to raise some issues, not to propose trichotomies or continua as especially virtuous or ideal types. Nor was it the intention of this present collection to establish 'everyday resistance' as a reified academic category comparable with 'peasant rebellion', nor as an anarchistic alternative to more romantic or vanguardist notions.

'In-between' in terms of *scale* of participation and collectivity, and degree of confrontation or forcefulness, draws attention to more widespread phenomena such as movement of population to government forest reserve land in defiance of authorities, or withdrawal or reallocation of labour (such as refusal to grow export crops), or the turning around of official forms of association to suit the perceived needs and aspirations of poor farmers. These may not be coordinated or planned in a full sense, and we must allow for the possibility of a number of independent or spontaneous initiatives adding up to a large-scale phenomenon, but it would be a mistake to underestimate the importance of popular styles and channels for sharing and disseminating information and experience and mutual decision-making. Moreover, local protest *mobilisation* using modern means of communication and transport clearly require a considerable degree of careful coordination and planning. These might include sit-ins in town centres – one case where pigs were driven into the courtyard of the provincial offices comes to mind – petitions backed by demonstrations and rallies with columns of vehicles, and so on.

'In-between' in terms of *time* is intended to focus attention on what, so to speak, with hindsight might be said to go on in-between major movements or uprisings, before and after or between one and the next. It focuses on the build-up before a major historical event, and on what happens after disappointment and defeat or possibly an only partial victory, to the personnel and fragments of organisation, ideas and programmes which survive.

'In-between' in the sense of *mediation* is an aspect of the previous senses and allows us to consider possible historical or potential links between quotidian and secular forms of struggle, or between local mobilisations and larger-scale social movements, and even insurgencies, whether those may be anticipated, nascent or already developed.

This focus on 'in-between' forms of resistance was suggested by a research intervention undertaken with members of poor farmers' organisations to reflect on their experience of regrouping and restarting after a period (approximately 1975–78) when there had been considerable suppression of peasant initiatives and during which a number of peasant leaders had been assassinated. The subsequent level of organisation and activity was relatively low, but in both quantity and quality it was certainly other than routine or uncoordinated. Much of what went on was not just the building of formal local associations and pressing economic demands, although these were initially foregrounded in our discussions. In practice poor farmers found equally important a whole range of discursive practices, conducted in their own specific style which insistently, if not always explicitly, challenged official definitions and constraints. Thus they found important *as forms of struggle* various informal means of meeting, travelling, linkage amongst themselves; of talking, sharing, learning and reflecting between poor rural producers in common situations. These were processes in which dignity and self-confidence were increased; experiences and useful knowledge were established, learned and shared; solidarity and material networks of personal links were developed; forms of communication, leadership and organisation were tried and tested; and alliances, however modest, were built up – some of them inter-class and supralocal.

Such forms of activity and cumulative experience are largely qualitative indices or achievements, not easily assessed, let alone measured. Farmers themselves none the less judged them to be symptomatically and substantively important. They are arguably a less vulnerable form of activity than more obviously militant, illegal or confrontational activity. And while in more critical and self-consciousness manifestations they may be thinly and unevenly spread throughout the country, they are ubiquitous in less self-conscious manifestations. They may constitute creative links between, on the one hand, those elements of peasant or popular culture and consciousness and local memories which we might want to call culture of resistance, produced in struggle and, on the other hand, new forms of culture, political ideas, etc. including those disseminated from other areas of society and especially relatively undominated or oppositional kinds of a more or less erudite nature, not excluding contributions made by solidary research interventions.

To use a military metaphor, those involved in these middle-range forms of struggle might be said to be engaged in a kind of 'patrolling' activity in a 'war of position' – as opposed to a 'war of movement' in which large-scale social forces are mobilised and confront each other in frequent, full-scale, mobile, head-on encounters. They are patrolling a middle-ground, and for those who imagine a future goal: in the meantime. If we develop the military metaphor, we can say that patrolling serves a variety of tactical functions and that while it is risky it incurs minimal losses. Patrolling serves to assert strength in contested territory held securely by neither side and to deny advantages to the opponent; it serves to test defences and to gather intelligence. It also serves to make contact with friendly forces, and to enhance morale and overcome fear. Of course, superordinate opponents also patrol the middle-ground, and have many advantages, but strategies of power are not the exclusive property of socially dominant forces. Nor do strategies necessarily require a coordinated plan or programme, but may also be seen as the exploitation of possibilities which various agents discern and create, synthesising heterogeneous elements [*Foucault*, 1980: 251].

The effects of such forms of popular resistance are not predictable or guaranteed, although in practice they are likely to be taken into account in tactical calculations. Optimistic peasant militants, with a specific goal of emancipation in mind, may claim, as did Salud Algabre, a woman who was involved in the organisation of the 1938 Sakdal peasant uprising in the Philippines, 30 years after the events, that 'No uprising fails. Each one is a step in the right direction.' (cited in Ileto [1979: 17]). Even a sympathetic commentator must add that not every step 'in the right direction' is taken without backward steps, nor is each step necessarily a further step; nor is each step necessarily on the same path among the many paths which might lead in the general direction intended. Yet in a longer-term historical, even human, perspective we might concede that the cumulative effect of popular resistance, and of attempts at going beyond, overcoming and transforming what is resisted, may be massive and decisive not least for the quality of future struggles which may lie ahead.

REFERENCES

Chatthip Nartsupha, 1984, 'The Ideology of "Holy Men" Revolts in North East Thailand', in Andrew Turton and Shigeharu Tanabe (eds.), *History and Peasant Consciousness in South East Asia*, Senri Ethnological Studies No. 13, Osaka: National Museum of Ethnology, pp. 111–34.
Foucault, Michel, 1980, *Power/Knowledge* (ed. Colin Gordon), Brighton: Harvester Press.
Giddens, Anthony, 1981, *A Contemporary Critique of Historical Materialism*, London: Macmillan.
Hirsch, Philip, 1985, 'Village into State and State into Village: The Rural Development Entry', paper presented to the Third Thai–European seminar, Thai Khadi Research Institute, Hua Hin, Thailand, April.
Hobsbawm, Eric and George Rudé, 1973, *Captain Swing*, Harmondsworth: Penguin Books.
Ileto, Reynaldo, 1979, *Pasyon and Revolution: Popular Movements in the Philippines 1840–1910*, Quezon City: Ateneo de Manila University Press.
Kanjana Kaewthep, 1984, 'Etude des "idéologies contre le pouvoir" des paysans thaïlandais au cours de la période 1973–1976', thèse pour le Doctorat de 3ème cycle, Université Paris 7.
Kanoksak Kaewthep, 1984, 'Les transformations structurelles et les conflits de classe dans la societé rurale thaïlandaise d'après l'étude d'un cas: La Féderation de la Paysannerie Thaïlandaise' (Farmers Federation of Thailand – FFT) (1973–1976), thèse pour le Doctorat de 3ème cycle, Université Paris 7.
Tanabe, Shigeharu, 1984, 'Ideological Practice in Peasant Rebellions: Siam at the Turn of the Twentieth Century', in Andrew Turton and Shigeharu Tanabe (eds.), *History and Peasant Consciousness in South East Asia*, Senri Ethnological Series No. 13, Osaka: National Museum of Ethnology, pp. 75–110.
Therborn, Göran, 1980, *The Ideology of Power and the Power of Ideology*, London: Verso Editions.

Turton, Andrew, 1984, 'Limits of Ideological Domination and the Formation of Social Consciousness', in Andrew Turton and Shigeharu Tanabe (eds.), *History and Peasant Consciousness in South East Asia*, Senri Ethnological Studies No. 13, Osaka: National Museum of Ethnology, pp. 19–73.
Turton, Andrew, 1985, 'Local Powers and Rural Differentiation', paper presented to the workshop on Agrarian Differentiation in South East Asia, Social Science Research Council, Chiangmai, Thailand, January.

Everyday Resistance, Socialist Revolution and Rural Development: The Vietnamese Case

Christine Pelzer White*

This article takes up two major themes which were discussed in the conference on 'Everyday forms of peasant resistance in South-east Asia' and further elaborated upon in the article by James Scott in this volume. The first is balancing the 'inordinate attention to large-scale peasant insurrection' with an examination of the role of everyday forms of peasant resistance in transforming social reality; the second is an examination of the relationship between the peasantry and the state in the post-revolutionary, post-colonial context.

The greatest merit of this approach is the focus it accords to the actions of peasants who are so often portrayed as led or determined by outside political and economic forces in the form of party leadership, state development programmes and capitalist or socialist transformation. As Scott argues:

> Any history or theory of peasant politics which attempts to do justice to the peasantry as an historical actor must necessarily come to grips with what I have chosen to call 'everyday forms of resistance'. For this reason alone it is important to both document and to bring some conceptual order to this seeming welter of human activity.

It is, of course, the task of social scientists to discover the hidden logic or 'laws of motion' which can impart sense to the miscellaneous acts and facts of everyday life. For Marxist political economists, class struggle is this basic organising principle; for neo-classical economists the fundamental dynamic is to be found in rational choices by economically motivated individuals. Scott's approach has the interesting originality of combining these two most influential contemporary paradigms: when peasants react in a utilitarian and individualistic fashion against the powerful forces destroying their lives they are also engaging in class struggle. In acting to marginally increase their chance for survival against devastating odds, they are also carrying out acts of resistance. Yes ... but when a peasant severs the fingers of his right hand in order to avoid conscription – a graphic example of individual peasant resistance which Scott cites from French history – he avoids death as a soldier, but at the cost of both his bodily integrity and his ability to produce for his own livelihood. Are acts of resistance which add up to self-sabotage

*Graduate School of International Studies, University of Denver, Denver, CO 80208, USA.

of the peasant's own creative energies and way of life – footdragging, self-mutilation, abandoning ancestral home and village to flee taxes and conscription – the best alternative open to peasants? Scott seems to answer this in the affirmative: he appears to hold no hope for a modern system which might operate to the peasants' *advantage*, for a system where the peasant might be an active citizen, not a protesting victim.

This is a sign of the times. In the 1960s and early 1970s there was a certain consensus on the left in the West that peasant revolution and national liberation struggle would open the way for a radically improved system for the rural population which constituted a viable alternative to capitalist transformation. It was argued that collectivisation in China and Vietnam improved peasant welfare in an egalitarian developmental context and demonstrated that a socialist state did not necessarily follow the Stalinist model of coercion *vis-à-vis* the peasantry.

To my mind, this still holds. But after the distressing spectacle in early 1979 of the Chinese People's Liberation Army destroying Vietnamese towns and villages in the northern border region so soon after American troops had done the same further south, and now that Vietnamese and Chinese peasant conscripts continue to fight and die on the frontier, some of the hope we had invested in peasant revolution has necessarily dimmed. Peasant revolution and successful national liberation does not usher in peace between socialist states; neither does it lead to the withering away of the state. However, this does not necessarily mean that the peasants have not achieved advantages as a result of revolutions and post-revolutionary agrarian reforms.

EVERDAY RESISTANCE OR CAPITALIST V. SOCIALIST RURAL DEVELOPMENT

The primary weakness of the 'everyday resistance' approach is its focus on negative manifestations of power rather than the question of how peasants can exercise positive political power. There are two successive ways of achieving the latter: first, overthrowing the exploitative system (and historically the power to do this has tended to come from a combination of armed struggle and political organisation rather than from low-key everyday resistance) and, second, peasant participation in the elaboration of a new system. There is no question that it is far more difficult to create a democratic, socialist system than to defeat colonialists and landlords, and in the absence of effective political means for the peasantry to express their own interests, the passive power of non-compliance with certain government policies may be the peasants' most effective method for forcing modifications in the new system (an insight derived from the 'everyday resistance' approach).

A further problem with Scott's approach is that the effectiveness of resistance is not considered of primary importance nor is it clearly specified what is being resisted (landlords? capitalism? the state?). As a result, dissimilar phenomena are grouped under the same rubric (for example, non-compliance with state development policies and a labour boycott against local landlords in protest against a deterioration in labour conditions). The conceptual slide from resistance to landlords to resistance to 'state policies' obscures the crucial question of the class content of state policies, that is, the differential impact of state policies on different rural classes and strata. Finally, Scott's use of the concept 'peasant' as a single, undifferentiated collective actor *vis-à-vis* landlords, the state, etc. ignores the crucial question of socio-economic differentiation between peasant households as well as differences in interest within peasant households which are especially acute in patriarchal systems. The concept 'peasants' applied to rural societies in both capitalist and socialist systems obscures the major differences between the two: capitalist development tends to increase the differentiation between peasant households in terms of landownership and access to labour, credit and inputs, while socialist development policies generally work to decrease differentiation, equalise access to the means of production and food and create a relatively homogeneous new class, 'the collective peasantry'.

Scott argues that revolution creates a more powerful state, to the detriment of the peasantry. Revolution, he claims:

> almost always creates a more coercive and hegemonic state apparatus – one that is often able to batten itself on the rural population like no other before it. All too frequently the peasantry finds itself in the ironic position of having helped to power a ruling group whose plans for industrialisation, taxation and collectivisation are very much at odds with the goals for which peasants had imagined they were fighting.

In fact, socialist states are often *weaker* in relationship to the peasantry than their capitalist counterparts because they have abolished powerful tools of economic coercion which operate in capitalist systems to drain the peasantry of the fruits of its labours: private ownership of land and uncontrolled markets in labour and food. While Stalin replaced economic coercion with the coercion of administrative pressure and violence, the Vietnamese state has not used the route of physical coercion. Many of Vietnam's present development problems stem from the fact that structural reforms – land reform and co-operativisation – have increased the power and standard of living of the peasantry to the extent that national accumulation from agriculture is severely curtailed.

Far from 'battening' on the rural population, during the food crisis of the late 1970s in Vietnam it was state officials who did not have enough to eat and got thinner and thinner while peasants grew enough to feed themselves, but not enough for the non-agricultural population. Furthermore, the Socialist Republic of Vietnam is not more coercive *vis-à-vis* the peasantry than its predecessors, the French colonial state and the American-backed Republic of Vietnam (South Vietnam). The economic and political violence of the colonial system has been well documented (for example, in Ngo Vinh

Long's *Before the Revolution*); the same applies for the use of military force as an instrument of state coercion by the Saigon government and its American allies. That the post-revolutionary Vietnamese state is more hegemonic than its predecessors means, among other things, that its authority has greater acceptance as legitimate, which is an essential precondition for a *less* coercive state.

It is by no means self-evident that industrialisation, taxation and collectivisation are at odds with the goals Vietnamese peasants fought for. The plans of the 'ruling group' helped to power by Vietnamese peasant revolutionaries include providing peasants with improved agricultural inputs and consumer goods through industrialisation, providing the peasant population with improved health and education and a national defence system, and creating a relatively economically undifferentiated peasant social structure with relatively equitable distribution of food and welfare through collectivisation. The egalitarian social and economic context created by Vietnamese co-operatives seems to me perfectly compatible with Scott's own definition of primary peasant concern for 'moral economy' (a priority to subsistence and the survival of the peasant way of life). If peasants reject profit maximising, economic differentiation, and rapid economic growth and accumulation at the price of a declining food and welfare entitlement for a sizeable portion of the population, as Scott argues in *The Moral Economy of the Peasant* (1976), then what Vietnamese peasants were fighting for shares many of the crucial elements of the Vietnamese state's aims and achievements in collectivisation.

A central assumption of Scott's peasant populism seems to be that the state is always and everywhere the enemy of the peasant, with no potential positive role to play. The most interesting process to study then becomes peasant resistance to what is generally conceptualised as 'development': mechanisation, capitalisation, the generation of marketable surplus, accumulation, etc. While this is in my view overly negative, it is a refreshing alternative to the vision of the growing field of 'rural development', which assumes that the state orchestrates rural change in an enlightened manner [*Lea and Chaudhri*, 1983]. State plans are often unrealistic and peasant non-compliance a valuable corrective. Here again there are significant differences between the policies of capitalist and socialist states. One potential outcome of the process of capitalist transformation of the agrarian sector in the Third World would be the emergence of a politically significant farmer class capable of obtaining significant advantages from the state, including high prices and price support systems for agricultural commodities and subsidised access to agricultural inputs in some variant of the North American and Western European model. Meanwhile, the bulk of the former peasant population becomes economically marginalised, forced into the desperate survival strategies of the rural poor or driven to find an alternative urbanised way of life as workers or urban slum dwellers.

Is there a democratic and socialist alternative to this dominant development pattern? Is it possible for peasants to enter the modern world as citizens rather than as passive subjects and victims? Can they enjoy benefits from nationally organised industrialisation and socio-economic transformation rather than suffer a deterioration of their previous standard of living and way of life? I believe that this is what the Vietnamese revolution has attempted to achieve, and although it has not succeeded there are insufficient grounds to bring out the familiar argument, 'revolution betrayed'.

APPLYING THE 'EVERDAY RESISTANCE' APPROACH TO VIETNAM

Many examples in modern Vietnamese history from colonial times to the present day could be fitted into the general rubric of 'everyday forms of peasant resistance'. Some are trivial but others have been of such importance as to rival the transformations brought about by armed rebellion and political revolution. This focus has much to offer in filling out the picture of peasant actions in their own class interest which were not limited, under colonial rule, to overpowered armed resistance or passive but increasingly resentful compliance – and which did not come to an end with the victory of a revolutionary party espousing the interests of the Vietnamese peasants and workers.

In the remainder of this article I will discuss a number of examples of such resistance and the insights to be gained. However, while focusing on the concept of 'everyday resistance' does help illuminate some important neglected aspects of rural socio-political dynamics, it does not advance us very far in the analysis of the power relationship between peasants and local and national power structures; in fact, it may obscure and mystify as much as it illuminates. The structure of power relations which determine the effectiveness or futility of resistance seems far more crucial than whether 'resistance' can be identified.

COLONIAL VIETNAM: EVERDAY RESISTANCE AND EVERYDAY COLLABORATION

The agrarian pattern in French Indo-China is well known: in Cochin-China, huge tracts of tenant-farmed riceland owned by French and collaborating Vietnamese beneficiaries of colonial land grants ('concessions'); in Tonkin and Annam, a complex situation characterised initially by tiny, fragmented holdings owned in part by peasant cultivators, in part by corporate villages in the form of communal land, and in part by relatively small landlords, but with a steady rise of land concentration under the impact of French colonial tax and land policies. An impression given by much of the literature is that this pattern was the outcome of the action of French colonial policy on pre-existing traditional rural life (the recent and relatively sparse Vietnamese settlement in the Mekong Delta; longer established 'closed' corporate landowning villages in the densely populated deltas of Annam and Tonkin). The colonial government or in some versions, the capitalism which it introduced, was the active agent; Vietnamese peasants, when not in active revolt, were passively embedded in the clay of nature, history and demography.

The main tendency in studies of the period of conquest and colonial rule has been to concentrate on elite response and on armed or overtly violent forms of struggle (for example, the excellent studies by Truong Buu Lam [1967] and David Marr [1971]). Mandarins surrendered, resisted or committed suicide; patriotic mavericks such as the strongman De Tham fought the good fight for years but were finally defeated; Annamese peasant demonstrators besieged administrators in crisis years (1908; 1930). The story seems to be that peasants charge into the fray of armed resistance when there is a crisis and a 'leader' or 'movement' to follow, but in between these heroic, if often futile, movements they keep their heads down and sullenly plough their furrows, harvest their rice and pay more and more of it in rent and/or taxes until the next 'precipitating crisis' (harvest failure, depression, war) and/or 'charismatic leader' comes along. This is not just the picture which emerges from studies published in the West; Vietnamese revolutionary historiography puts a great deal of emphasis on the role of the leader, the 'vanguard party', and the 'opportune moment'.

A change of focus to 'everyday forms of peasant resistance' allows a different picture to form in which, at first glance at least, peasant action is more central. Pierre Gourou's work on the Tonkin delta provides one example: peasants, hostile to the break in local custom involved when an outsider acquired some land in the village, made sure that the 'usurped' field would be barren of rice by surreptitiously drawing a string across the field in spring. [*Gourou*, 1955]. However, although such sabotage may have slowed down the process of peasant land loss in the Tonkin delta, it did not ultimately prevent steady peasant pauperisation and the rise of landlordism during the course of the colonial period. Like many other instances of literal and figurative footdragging, much low-key resistance seems to have actually functioned primarily as delaying tactics in an inexorable process of peasant loss of land.

However, at least one effective but ignored instance of peasant resistance radically transformed French colonial land policy in Tonkin. During the period of conquest, the widespread form of peasant non-violent resistance was flight to the foothills, deserting fields and villages to the advancing French. The colonial response was to sell or give away these 'empty' lands as huge concessions to French colons [*Thompson*, 1937: 145–6]. There were grandiose plans to turn Tonkin into a settler colony along the lines of Quebec; one French writer even wrote that 'Tonkin will doubtless be able to furnish us wheat as cheaply as North America'! [cited in *Robequain*, 1944: 191]. In 1900, the threshold between the decades of 'conquest' and the period of 'colonial development', *two-thirds* of the land in Vietnam which had been given or sold as concessions to French colons was in Tonkin; only one-fourth was in Cochin-China [*Nguyen Khac Dam*, 1957: 74]. The policy of turning Tonkin into a settler colony or setting up the kind of large absentee landlord system which later emerged in Cochin-China foundered on the reef of peasant resistance in Tonkin; in the words of a leading historian of the colonial period: 'there was a shortage of labour since the ousted Annamites naturally refused to work the land of those whom they regarded as usurpers' [*Thompson*, 1937: 145–6]. The colonial government faced pressure from colons demanding that the government buy back the land they could not put into cultivation for lack of willing labourers, while in other cases peasant resistance to the colons erupted into violent struggle, which made the government find it politic to restore the peace by returning the land to the villagers who felt so strongly that it was theirs by right. By the early 1930s the remaining pockets of concessions in Tonkin were historical relics – Pierre Gourou, in his survey of the Tonkin delta, described one concentration of huge concessions of as much as 700 hectares each as 'evidence of an unfortunate policy which has now been definitely abandoned' [*Gourou*, 1955: 254].

In Cochin-China, however, the same policy was neither pronounced 'unfortunate' nor abandoned. In other words, Tonkin peasant resistance had a decisive influence on the course of colonial policy and the emerging agrarian pattern of French-ruled Vietnam at the beginning of this century.

Peasants resisted, peasants guided the hand of history, peasants defeated government policy; but this is only part of the story. When we turn to the question of how to conceptualise this resistance, it is not possible to describe it as straightforward anti-colonial resistance. For example, many of the peasants who refused to farm for colons on what had been their own land found alternative employment – building the roads, railroads and administrative buildings which went up in the early colonial years. French settler farmers were competing for labour with the colonial public works programme. Tonkin peasants may have effectively resisted French pipe-dreams of turning Tonkin into a settler colony by refusing to be their tenants, but as construction workers they helped transform Governor-General Paul Doumer's visionary blueprint for French Indo-China into reality.

We find a similar situation when the local population near fledgling rubber plantations in Cochin-China proved unusable as estate workers. The montagnards were not accustomed to an intensive work schedule, could easily flee, and resented French land occupation on what had been part of their territory for slash-and-burn agriculture. Tonkinese peasants, however, broken into the discipline of long work hours by the intensive rice cultivation of the most densely populated provinces of the Red River delta, and duped by the enticements of labour recruiters, were brought in as the plantation labour force [*Boserup*, 1965].

Perhaps the lesson of these cases is that resistance is stronger when peasants are asked to work the same land in worse conditions than when the place and type of work are radically different from past experience.

If the peasant majority is held to play a major role in the making of history, then established rule, however oppressive and exploitative, depends in large measure upon their collaboration or compliance with the system.

Therefore we must add an inventory of 'everyday forms of peasant *collaboration*' to balance our list of 'everyday forms of peasant resistance': both exist, both are important. I suspect, moreover, that in 'normal' periods there is more everyday collaboration than everyday resistance. Indeed, this is why new regimes seek rapid 'normalisation'.

For established rulers or elites, everyday forms of resistance constitute the major problem, for once open rebellion is repressed or kept in check the only resistance left is footdragging, absenteeism and all the other weapons of the weak and unorganised whose capacity for strong resistance has been broken. However, some such 'resistance' in fact functions often as a safety valve: for example, the harmless village play in which the permanently poor and helpless take comfort in scenes of role reversal or in mockery of their 'betters' (a term closer to 'elites' than to, for example, 'oppressors' or 'exploiters'). There are always little ways in which rent or tax-paying peasants can 'cheat' or 'trick' the landlord or government. But note the lack of legitimacy implied in these terms, unlike the mobilisation to righteous struggle which accompanies peasant or nationalist uprisings. In cases where the peasants are resigned to accepting the system, putting energy into ruses to marginally 'cheat' the system can mask the unpalatable fact that in fact it is they who are being royally exploited, that is, 'cheated'. The tricks of adding stones, straw, etc. to increase the weight of the landlord or tax collector's share of the harvest can perhaps give peasants the illusion of having more power and manoeuvrability than is actually the case – that is, these ineffective but psychologically satisfying forms of resistance could in fact contribute to false consciousness, blinding people to the painful reality of the extent of their powerlessness and exploitation.

A further problem with this concept of everyday forms of resistance is the very formulation: it is those in authority, the landlords or the government, who label such acts 'resistance'. The peasant furtively cheating on the weight of the harvest is just trying to get as much as possible out of a raw deal – I doubt that it is often thought of as a mini-rebellion. It is the established authorities, if they find it out, who treat it and punish it as such. For example, in the film about life on an Italian peasant estate, 'Tree of the Wooden Clogs', the motivation for the central dramatic act of cutting down a tree is not defiance of the landlord's authority but, rather, that a peasant boy's clog had split and in his impoverished situation his father saw no other way to obtain another clog. It was the landlord who chose to interpret this as an act of resistance to established authority and expel the hapless peasant family from his estate.

From the point of view of a revolutionary who wants to transform the system, the most salient fact, the central problem, is the degree of peasant compliance with and acceptance of the system which exploits them. For instance, in *The Peasant Question*, Communist Party organisers Truong Chinh and Vo Nguyen Giap report a conversation with a tenant:

We asked: 'The landlord collects half of the produce as rent at harvest time: is this exploitation?' The tenant replied, 'You can't really call it exploitation. I don't own any land, so I am lucky that he rents to me. I can farm, and he owns land, so of course it is just that each of us gets half of the harvest' (p. 22).

This same real or imagined symbolic tenant probably put as much straw in the landlord's half as he could get away with, and might have roared with laughter at impersonations of the landlord at village shows. He might even have made up a satirical ditty about the landlord's personal quirks and habits. But in the balance of his actions he goes along with the rules of the system and his consciousness is nowhere near conceptualising the necessity, or even possibility, of a change of system. In this sense, he collaborates in maintaining the system.

This is not to say that 'everyday forms of resistance' cannot be significant in peasant involvement in a revolutionary movement. One example comes from the memoirs of a man who, as a peasant youth with a smattering of education in 1930, first heard of communism through contemporary newspaper accounts of 'communist rebels' in Nghe-Tinh. Without any other information or contact, he called together a group of friends and proposed that they consider themselves 'communists' and stand up to the rich and powerful of the village. He suggested that those who work for the rich fight back against beatings and sabotage the landlords' buffaloes on the sly by beating them under the legs so as not to leave any tell-tale marks. When they worked in the landlords' kitchens they should throw leftovers to the dogs lest they be used for the meals of other agricultural labourers and when harvesting for the landlords always leave paddy in the field for poor children to glean [*Chanh Thi*, 1960]. After a while they were successful in putting an end to beatings at the village *dinh* previously considered a 'village custom', and this had a demonstration effect on the poor in neighbouring villages and attracted the attentions of a Communist Party organiser who recruited this group as a cell in the wider party network.

Such resistance to the rich and powerful organised in small peasant communities as well as on a regional scale existed in other colonised Southeast Asian countries, and has existed periodically among poor peasants and landless labourers in post-colonial South-east Asia to this day. What are the conditions necessary for such scattered and low-key resistance to lead to a revolutionary transformation of the rural socio-economic system? In Vietnam, the route included peasant involvement in a revolutionary alliance with other social groups, most notably intellectuals but also workers, and culminated in the DRV land reform of 1953–56 [*White*, 1974; 1979]. The land reform campaign explicitly aimed at redistributing not only land but also power from the landlords and rural elite to the majority of the peasantry (the former landless, poor peasants, and middle peasants). Although the process of redistribution of power was more problematic than the redistribution of land, the economic and political power of the former landlord class was broken once and for all, and a significant number of peasants from poor and landless class backgrounds (if not the class as a whole) were promoted to local positions of responsibility and gained political experience [*White*, 1981]. In my view, the shift of power achieved in the land reform was consolidated through the formation of co-operatives which ensured the peasants access to land and employment, both on a collective and family basis: membership in the co-operative guaranteed peasants both employment on the co-operative land and access to an inalienable family plot. While not providing prosperity, the new post-revolutionary co-operative socio-economic system provided an improved standard of living and relatively egalitarian access to employment, land and rice which had not existed under the colonial state.

REVOLUTION BETRAYED?

The case that socialist countries are just as anti-peasant as the others has been put most forcefully in Michael Lipton's study of 'urban bias in world development' [*Lipton*, 1977] while the argument that peasant interests are at odds with those of the party is a theme in James Scott's *The Moral Economy of the Peasant* [*Scott*, 1976] as well as in his article in this volume. Are the pre- and post-revolutionary systems in Vietnam radically different, that is, has a real agrarian revolution taken place? Is the peasant always and everywhere condemned to a weak and defensive position of resistance against more powerful local elites and the state, whether that state be labelled 'capitalist' or 'socialist' and the local elites called 'landlords and rich farmers' or 'cadres'?

My short answer is that, despite some similarities, there are extremely important differences between pre- and post-revolutionary Vietnam. Of course, except in relatively industrialised countries where agricultural subsidies have been introduced, most states try to extract more surplus than agricultural producers are willing to part with. Even in the Third World there are exceptions, such as when the Republic of Vietnam's budget was provided primarily by US aid and therefore it was not necessary to squeeze the South Vietnamese peasantry fiscally. But widespread peasant reluctance to meet government tax and procurement demands seems less significant than the differences in methods employed in different states to overcome this resistance. In colonial Vietnam pressure on peasants who did not come up with the required head tax included, literally, the use of thumbscrews; the Vietnamese socialist government's methods are limited to administrative pressures, emulation campaigns and unfavourable rural–urban terms of trade embodied in official prices of agricultural and industrial commodities.

The major problems for the peasantry during the colonial period were its inability, despite the forms of 'everyday resistance' mentioned earlier, to prevent loss of their land, and growing hunger as the lion's share of rice production left the villages as a result of economic pressures backed up by the use of force where necessary. In the 1970s, on the other hand, the major problem for socialist government policy was growing *peasant* encroachment on co-operative land and the government's inability to induce the peasants to grow and deliver enough surplus to feed the cities. To me this indicates a very considerable shift in the balance of power in the new system in the direction of the peasantry.

EVERYDAY FORMS OF PEASANT RESISTANCE AND SOCIALIST AGRARIAN POLICY

In post-revolutionary Vietnam what could be called peasant everyday resistance – or non-compliance with official policy – has been a major constraint on the effectiveness of state economic planning and agrarian policy. To take one example, it has been government policy to keep the price of rice low. It was felt to be a principle of socialism that the basic foodgrain should not be a commodity. There should be no free market in a basic human necessity; no cash nexus governing full and empty stomachs. It was a major policy aim to insulate this basic necessity from the 'law of value' and to relate the circulation of rice to a combination of need and work through the complicated workings of the rural co-operative, procurement and urban rationing systems. In the initial years, this system worked reasonably well, although never perfectly; it seems to have broken down under a combination of the pressures of war which caused rapid inflation in free market prices and the sudden reduction in foreign aid after the end of the war and deterioration of relations with China. Shortfalls in state rations due to procurement difficulties, and the high price of rice on the free market caused hardship for state employees and urban workers on fixed salaries.

Peasants unhappy about the procurement price of rice, and the lack of availability of consumer goods in exchange, had many ways of resisting official exhortations to increase production and deliveries to the state: for example, by reducing the amount of energy expended by restricting the acreage of co-operative rice land or refusing to harvest some of it (some land as well as much energy was transferred to the 'family economy' which was centred on the five per cent of co-operative land reserved for household use) or by transforming the low-priced commodity rice into a more profitable and more easily marketable commodity by feeding it to ducks or pigs, distilling it into alcohol, etc. Experimentation since the Sixth Plenum in 1979 with a more liberal pricing and marketing system is in part a result of peasant dissatisfaction with, and 'resistance' to the earlier system. (For a discussion of the Sixth Plenum, see Nguyen huu Dong [1981] and White [1983].)

However, it should be noted that the same phenomena could be used as illustrations for rather different theories. What I have mentioned here as an example of peasant 'resistance' to government policy could equally well be cited as an example of rational peasant economic calculation, that is, either Scott or Popkin in the terms of the 'moral economy' v. 'rational peasant' debate [*Scott*, 1976; *Popkin*, 1979]. Focus on the motivation of individual or collective peasant action, it seems to me, tends to homogenise peasant action under *different* political economic systems: whether the system is feudal, capitalist or socialist, peasants always resist the state and the local elite; peasants always make rational economic calculations. What seems more interesting is to understand the systemic differences in the contexts in which these peasant responses (or calculations) take place which vary in very significant ways between colonial and post-colonial capitalist states as well as between the colonial capitalist system and the post-colonial transition to socialism in the case of Vietnam.

ANALYSING RURAL POWER RELATIONS

I would like to outline what I see as the main elements necessary for an analysis and comparative study of rural power relations and their trans-formations.

(1)   At least four levels need to be distinguished, and the powers of each within the system defined: the state (divided into national and regional levels); the 'local elite' (village government, landlords, party cadres as the case may be); peasant households and individuals within these households. The last is crucial in order to take account of gender and generational differences among the peasantry. The field of peasant studies generally implicitly equates 'the peasant' with male household heads, which actually excludes the majority of the peasant population from the socio-economic analysis. This is important for the analysis of 'peasant resistance' as house-hold heads and other household members do not necessarily have the same interests. This is especially true in a peasant family farming system where the household head owns the land and controls family labour. For example, in the move from a system of primarily male controlled 'family farms' to a co-operative form of agriculture there are cases in which within the same household the wife was enthusiastic about the idea of collective work but the husband was more resistant to the new co-operative policy. One case study of a Vietnamese village found that in the initial stage of co-operativisation the family land was divided in half and husbands and wives chose separately whether or not to join the co-operative [*Pham Cuong and Nguyen Van Ba*, 1976: 35; *White*, 1982]. In other words, there can be both 'resistance' and support for a government policy within a single peasant household.

(2)   Following on from the previous point, one can then analyse the patterns of alliance between the various actors: the state and the peasantry against the local elite (anti-landlord in the land reform; anti-local cadre corruption in socialist reform campaigns), the peasants and the local elite against the state (for example, in either the traditional or socialist corporate village to keep payments to the state at a minimum); the state and in-dividuals against household heads (in the case of the marriage law, and in the above-mentioned case of conflict between husbands and wives over sup-

porting the government's co-operative programme), or against corrupt or overbearing local officials.

(3) To what extent is it possible to transform a sovereign state–subject peasant system in which the only choice open to the peasantry is compliance or resistance to policies imposed from the outside? In some political systems (multi-party electoral as in Malaysia; the Vietnamese political process of leading party, mass organisations, elections and democratic centralism) is it meaningful to describe peasants as citizens and not merely subjects, unlike colonial and post-colonial military regimes which rely heavily on the use of force *vis-à-vis* the peasantry? In terms of Vietnamese ideological aims, is it possible for peasants to become 'collective masters' of the society?

(4) Phenomena which can appear as 'individual' or 'spontaneous' and unorganised resistance are probably often rooted in structures, such as collective cultural beliefs and habits or patterns of old or new economic exchanges, which are not sufficiently recognised or understood. Some theories concerning these patterns have been advanced: Scott in *Moral Economy* analyses peasant resistance to colonial transformations in terms of well-established economic cultural norms concerning subsistence and reciprocity. Another such pattern hypothesised by Ester Boserup is that the interaction of demography and agricultural technology produces culturally enshrined patterns of work and leisure which are very resistant to change. In the case of Vietnam, I find this helpful in understanding the difficulty in implementing government programmes involving labour intensification (increasing the number of harvests per year, moving from extensive slash-and-burn agriculture to more labour-intensive sedentary agriculture in the highlands. The government campaign for introducing a third harvest per year, an early spring rice crop, places a peak labour demand right at *Tet*, the traditional long yearly holiday which used to correspond with a long agricultural slack season but which in the new more intensive agricultural calendar is already much curtailed.

These patterns need not, however, be only remnants of the past but also include new emerging forms of patterned but 'unofficial' economic exchanges. For example, much of what has appeared as 'corruption' or 'illegal activity' in Vietnam actually could be better analysed as forms of exchange between individual or collective actors dealing with each other directly rather than through official government channels. For example, an electricity station agreed to provide electricity to a co-operative in exchange for a stipulated number of pigs and chickens for the electricity station workers. Formally, such an exchange was illegal; informally, it could be seen as a more direct worker–peasant exchange than the official channel of state procurement from co-operatives and state wages and rations for the workers. It only hit the newspapers in the form of a complaint about corruption when the electricity station failed to live up to its side of the bargain. In short, rather than calling such phenomena 'resistance' to official government policies and legal codes, they can be analysed as an emerging alternative structure of economic exchange. The economic reforms in Vietnam since 1979 could be analysed as an attempt to legalise a number of previously illegal but widespread and uncontrollable patterns of economic activity rooted in petty commodity production. The official economic system which had relied heavily on bureaucratic planning has had to be modified in light of the growing unofficial system of economic exchanges.

CONCLUSION

In the final analysis, accepting 'everyday resistance' as the primary framework for analysis depends on one's definition of peasant interests, and of the desirability of petty commodity production as a way of life to be defended for its own sake, as a high moral value. However, peasants do not necessarily want to remain peasants, and do not necessarily place highest priority on preserving their status as poor petty commodity producers in a richer world. Peasants frequently have the ambition of becoming non-peasants (whether for themselves or for their children): to become members of higher income or higher status groups, whether landlords, businessmen, white-collar workers, state employees, workers, teachers, etc. Vietnamese development thinking sees petty commodity production as the root of poverty, and industrialisation and technological change as the key to a better life for the whole population. If this is defined, as Scott seems to, as inimical to a core peasant desire to resist all outside attempts to destroy the petty commodity producing traditional way of life, then 'peasant interests' and state development plans are inexorably at odds. The dilemma which the Vietnamese system is attempting to solve is how to transform an economy of poor petty commodity producers into 'collective masters' of a more productive, prosperous and technologically advanced rural economic system. The reinvigoration of the peasant household economy and collective village institutions which were the result of structural reforms in Vietnam have increased peasants' power to defend what they see as their interests in this process of socio-economic transformation.

REFERENCES

Boserup, Ester, 1965, *The Conditions of Agricultural Growth*, London: Allen & Unwin.
Chanh Thi, 1960, 'Roi ba duoc vao Dang' (And then I joined the Party) in *Len duong thang loi: Hoi ky cach mang* (On the road to victory: Revolutionary memoirs), Hanoi: Van Hoc.
Gourou, Pierre, 1955, *The Peasants of the Tonkin Delta*, New Haven: HRAF.
Harriss, J., 1982, *Rural Development: Theories of Peasant Economy and Agrarian Change*, London: Hutchinson.
Lea, David, and D.P. Chaudhri, 1983, *Rural Development and the State*, London: Methuen.
Lipton, Michael, 1977, *Why Poor People Stay Poor: Urban Bias in World Development*, London: Temple Smith.

Marr, David, 1971, *Vietnamese Anticolonialism*, Berkeley: University of California Press.

Ngo Vinh Long, 1973, *Before the Revolution: The Vietnamese Peasants under the French*, Cambridge, MA: MIT Press.

Nguyen huu Dong, 1981, '6e plenum: adaptations conjoncturelles ou reformes durables? Essai sur la politique economique du socialisme', *Vietnam* (Paris), No. 2, April, pp. 41–60.

Nguyen Khac Dam, 1957, *Nhung thu doan boc lot cua tu ban Phap o Viet-Nam* (French capitalism's methods of exploitation in Vietnam), Hanoi: Nha Xuat Ban Van Su Dia.

Pham Cuong and Nguyen van Ba, 1976, *Revolution in the Village: Nam Hong, 1945–1975*, Hanoi: FLPH.

Popkin, Samuel, 1979, *The Rational Peasant: The Political Economy of Rural Society in Vietnam*, Berkeley: University of California Press.

Robequain, Charles, 1944, *The Economic Development of French Indochina*, London: Oxford University Press.

Scott, James, 1976, *The Moral Economy of the Peasant: Rebellion and Subsistence in Southeast Asia*, New Haven: Yale University Press.

Thompson, Virginia, 1937, *French Indochina*, New York: Macmillan.

Truong Buu Lam, 1967, *Patterns of Vietnamese Response to Foreign Intervention*: 1858–1900 (Monograph series No. 11), New Haven: Southeast Asian Studies, Yale University.

Truong Chinh and Vo Nguyen Giap, 1974, *The Peasant Question (1937–1938)* (data paper No. 94), Ithaca, NY: Southeast Asia Program, Cornell University.

White, Christine, 1974, 'The Vietnamese Revolutionary Alliance: Intellectuals, Workers and Peasants' in John W. Lewis (ed.), *Peasant Rebellion and Communist Revolution in Asia*, Stanford, CA: Stanford University Press.

White, Christine, 1979, 'The Peasants and the Party in the Vietnamese Revolution', in D.B. Miller (ed.) *Peasants and Politics: Grassroots Reactions to Change in Asia*, London: Edward Arnold.

White, Christine, 1981, *Agrarian Reform and National Liberation in the Vietnamese Revolution: 1920–1957*, Ann Arbor: University Microfilms.

White, Christine, 1982, 'Socialist Transformation of Agriculture and Gender relations: The Vietnamese Development Policy', in G. White, R. Murray and C. White (eds.), *Revolutionary Socialist Development in the Third World*, Brighton: Wheatsheaf.

From Footdragging to Flight: The Evasive History of Peasant Avoidance Protest in South and South-east Asia

Michael Adas*

In the late 1840s, large numbers of peasants from the Demak and Grobogan areas of the Semarang Residency on Java's north-east coast fled from their villages which were situated in areas where the Dutch had introduced the forced production of tobacco in the previous decade. In March of 1850, Dutch officials questioned a group of refugee peasants in an attempt to determine the grievances that had led to their flight and, if possible, convince them to return to their home villages, where severe labour shortages were making a shambles of colonial production quotas. After repeated assurances that they would not be harmed if they spoke freely, the refugees (or a particularly vocal and courageous one; it is not clear from accounts of the inquiry) related a long list of grievances. They claimed that they had once lived in a state of well-being that had been undermined by the introduction of the compulsory cultivation of tobacco which was one of the most demanding and time-consuming of the export crops that the Dutch collected in the era of the Cultivation System. The peasants' complaints – excessive production quotas, the disruption of rice cropping routines, intermittent demands for special services for which there was little or no pay, forced deliveries of tobacco at far below its market price – included many of the critical defects that Dutch pamphleteers cited in their hotly fought campaigns beginning in the 1840s to reform or abolish altogether the Cultivation System [*Fasseur*, 1978]. The peasants asserted that their families had been threatened by starvation as a result of the excessive demands of Dutch and Javanese officials. They fled in order to survive. They declared that they would not return unless the Dutch promised that they would no longer have to grow tobacco. In fact, in succeeding years many of these same peasants migrated *en masse* yet again in response to Dutch attempts to re-establish their control and reintroduce the compulsory production of export crops into the areas where the peasants had originally taken refuge [*Pierson*, 1868: 153–5; *Soest*, 1869: 3, 205].

These events – the large-scale flight of Javanese peasants and the impromptu Dutch inquiry – provide a rare instance of avoidance protest in

* *Department of History, Rutgers University, New Brunswick, NJ 08903, USA. My thanks to the members of the Hague workshop for their helpful comments and suggestions for revision.*

which peasant dissent was not merely recorded by government officials, but those who committed the acts of protest were given the opportunity to explain the motives for their resistance in some detail. If we assume that the peasants' responses were reasonably accurately recorded – admittedly a problematical supposition – it is possible to gain a sense of the more fundamental values and underlying sense of justice by which they evaluated the elite demands and defined the grievances that provoked their dissidence. The peasants' mistrust of all officials ('De kleine man klagt nooit openlijk');[1] their conviction that subsistence cultivation must take precedence over production for state or market demands; their belief that a man's labour ought to be fairly rewarded (even by the state); and their deep-seated belief that flight was an effective, although costly, means of combatting the excessive demands of local and colonial officials, are all readily apparent in the refugees' angry responses to the Dutch inquiry. The peasants' flight itself was an act of defence; Dutch questions had tranformed it into a vehicle for social protest.

Even in this 'best case' situation, the perils of avoidance protest as a subject of historical inquiry are strikingly illustrated. Careful examination of the questions asked and the peasants' replies reveals a wide range of problems relating to this rather rare encounter between European officials and peasant dissidents. Were the Dutch officials posing the right questions? To what degree were the questions posed and the responses actually recorded shaped by the Dutch administrators' personal feelings about the Cultivation System which was the object of great controversy at the time. Were the Javanese, whose mistrust of even apparently sympathetic officials is clear from their testimony, expressing their feelings fully or concealing deeper grudges and motives, or alternatively personal shortcomings and animosities that may have driven them to flee? In the available published accounts of this incident, we are told little about the composition of the peasant groups which fled or even the actual numbers involved. We do not know what measures they may have taken short of migration to defend themselves; why some peasants fled and others chose to remain; why the former migrated to the areas where the Dutch found them; or whether or not they considered more confrontational modes of protest, including those involving violence, as alternative means of countering what they perceived to be exploitative demands. These and other questions arise even in this instance where we have relatively hard evidence. For most incidents of avoidance protest the evidence is much more sketchy; the process of interpretation necessarily based more heavily on inference and speculation.

In recent years those who work with peasant social systems in a variety of disciplines have in a sense rediscovered these critical modes of protest for they have long been a central concern of those who study plantation societies or agrarian systems based on serfdom.[2] From passing references to foot-dragging or evasive protest as precursors of major riots or rebellions, we have moved (perhaps too quickly) to the position that these forms of 'dissent from within' [*Last*, 1970: 350ff] have been major – perhaps the most pervasive – modes of peasant protest to excessive elite demands. The importance of this shift in perspective cannot be overemphasised, for it may ultimately force a major rethinking of our approaches to the study of social protest, both rural and urban, more generally. Because they are embedded in established institutions and ongoing exchanges between patrons and clients at various levels, serious analysis of peasant defences and avoidance protest forces us to deal with *whole* social and political systems,[3] rather than concentrating on peasant conditions and responses to vaguely delineated and caricatured elites. It requires that we examine in depth the ongoing interaction and day-to-day contests over scarce resources between elites and peasants, taking into account the impact of institutions and ideologies on these processes. The study of peasant resistance in this wider perspective cannot be successfully accomplished unless we break down crude categories like elite/peasant and coloniser/colonised in order to unravel the complex layering of socio-economic hierarchies in rural societies and identify the bewildering varieties of exchanges and responses between individuals and groups at different levels. This approach accentuates the vertical dimensions of rural socio-political and economic relations, centred on patron–client interaction [*Scott*, 1972a, 1972b; *Scott and Kerkvliet*, 1973], and may force us to alter the way we look at peasant communities which, as Jan Breman has recently argued [1982], were more likely to have been elite-infiltrated and deeply divided by factions and variations in wealth than the closed, corporate entities that are often assumed in the literature on peasant societies.[4] Serious study of avoidance protest requires that we examine more fully the important links that have existed between ongoing or quasi-institutionalised modes of peasant resistance and specific outbursts of rural riot or rebellion, as well as the connections between peasant movements as different points in time.

An approach to peasant resistance that emphasises ongoing defences and modes of avoidance protest may well lead to the conclusion that, contrary to the impression conveyed by the great attention given in recent decades to rural conflict and peasant risings, outbursts of confrontational protest are exceptional occurrences and riots and rebellions are rare events, and revolutions even more so. This realisation will in turn require major alterations in the approaches that have dominated peasant protest studies for decades – studies in which topics are selected, arguments premised, and data organised on the assumption that the history of whole societies over considerable periods of time was inexorably shaped by and targeted towards major outbursts of societal conflict. Not only is this perspective narrow and crisis-centric; it promotes a wrong-headed approach to historical analysis – backwards from conflicts and confrontations that are viewed in retrospect as 'main events'.

In our enthusiasm to embrace this new vision of the dynamics of agrarian societies and peasant social protest, we should exercise great caution. We should do so not because this is a less viable way to study rural history than the major confrontation approach, but because the sources available for the study of the protest of avoidance, at least those extant for the pre-independence period, are limited and often difficult to interpret with precision or even the assurance that the investigator has understood the real meaning of the invariably scanty information that is available. The paucity and low quality of the source materials dealing with peasant defences and avoidance protest compounds the difficulties that would be encountered even if better documentation were available. The problems of distinguishing peasant defences from peasant protest and individual acts of resistance from reprisals resulting from personal quarrels; of determining whether peasant activities like banditry and arson are criminal acts or expressions of *social* protest; or of analysing the links between avoidance protest and peasant/ elite confrontations are greatly complicated by the lack of sufficient information.

The many problems associated with the study of rural protest, beginning with the scarcity of sources produced by peasants themselves, that have been identified by numerous authors are greatly magnified in the analysis of avoidance resistance because incidents of peasant footdragging or evasive reprisals are very likely not to have been recorded at all. The success of this form of protest has often depended on its clandestine nature. Officials must be deceived; 'cheating' must pass unnoticed, or at least its perpetrators must remain undiscovered. In addition, measures and activities that state officials condemned as illegal were often viewed by members of village communities as essential defences or just retribution for elite excesses and thus 'covered up'. In many instances, local officials themselves collaborated with village leaders or local men of influence to resist state demands for tribute or manpower. The collusion, deception and subterfuge that have been central to most forms of avoidance protest serve to frustrate the eager social scientists' efforts to understand this form of resistance every bit as much as they made it difficult for state officials to detect and punish it.

Even if evidence of peasant cheating or reprisal reached local or regional officials, it is likely to have been suppressed. In both the pre-colonial and colonial periods, the superiors of local officials were likely to view expressions of peasant unrest as signs of administrative incompetence or corruption on the part of their subordinates. Due to the disruptions that resulted and the need for military support from the court or district centre in times of violent peasant risings, it was virtually impossible to conceal incidents of confrontational protest, however much local leaders may have wished to cover them up. Pilfering, arson, crop concealment, adulterated tribute deliveries, verbal abuse and gestures of contempt, on the other hand, could be overlooked or dealt with by a local leader's hired toughs. If these expressions of discontent and resistance were reported, an official's reputation and career could be badly damaged or he could be exposed to attacks by his rivals. Evidence of misrule could bring dismissal, imprisonment or in some instances – as in seventeenth-century Burma [*Than Tun*, 1968: 177–80] – execution. Even if they reported incidents of avoidance protest, threatened and obviously hostile officials were unlikely to relate accurately the grievances, demands or aspirations of peasants driven to flight, footdragging or sectarian withdrawal.

The evasive, often clandestine, nature of most forms of avoidance protest means that there has historically been a very low ratio between the number of occurrences of this mode of dissent and those that have actually been recorded, much less described in detail. It is impossible to estimate this ratio with any precision, but it varied widely by time period, area, type of regime, and according to the form of protest involved from rarely recorded (but perhaps ubiquitous) incidents of peasant footdragging to frequently recorded instances of peasant protest migration *en masse*. The available evidence, however, makes it possible to delineate several broad categories of avoidance protest and to discern the conditions that caused them to change over time. Often the conditions that influenced peasant decisions to adopt particular forms of avoidance protest also have had a bearing on the extent to which these expressions of agrarian dissidence were recorded. The 'soft' state structures and poor communications systems of pre-colonial South and South-east Asian societies, for example, provided openings for a wide range of peasant avoidance responses. Low population-to-land ratios, the presence of large tracts of unoccupied land, and vigorous elite competition for limited supplies of manpower reinforced these tendencies and at the same time led to an official obsession with large-scale protest migrations or the transfer of peasant services from one elite patron to another. This concern resulted in fairly abundant documentation of these peasant responses. In the colonial era, detailed official reports on small-scale sectarian movements like those which made possible works like Drewes' classic account of Javanese chiliasm [*Drewes*, 1925], reflected the great anxiety felt by colonial officials regarding this sort of activity which they little understood or cared to tolerate. Better bookkeeping, improved communications and tighter bureaucratic control in the colonial period also forced peasants to rely more heavily on different forms of resistance than those they had favoured in the pre-colonial era and produced the sorts of records that make it possible for us to study elusive modes of protest like concealment, arson, feigned ignorance and production boycotts in some depth for the first time.

The bulk of this study is focused on an examination of the historical and situational factors in pre-colonial and colonial South and South-east Asia that influenced peasant preferences for different forms of avoidance protest and also often determined the extent to which these activities would be recorded. For the purpose of analysis, I have grouped the many forms of non-confrontational or avoidance resistance into three main types: (1) the protest of denial – everyday resistance; (2) the protest of denial – exit; and (3) the protest of retribution. The major distinction between types one and two, both of which are centred on the efforts of peasant cultivators to deny material resources or labour services to local notables or government officials whose demands are viewed as excessive, are structural. Modes of the protest of denial belonging to the first type are endemic to rural social systems and occur on an ongoing, day-to-day basis. Avoidance protest of the second type, which involves flight or transfer of peasant services and loyalties, are more dramatic and perilous and thus more rarely adopted by hardpressed peasants, usually when everyday defences are not sufficient to hold elite exactions at a tolerable level. As its name implies, in contrast to either type of the protest of denial, the protest of retribution consists of modes of peasant resistance that involve attempts to strike back at those who are viewed as sources of oppression. As distinguished from modes of confrontational protest, such as riots or rebellion, however, these forms of avoidance protest centre on anonymous reprisals or clandestine acts that are not intended to bring on direct confrontations between dissident tenants or labourers and those who are the targets of their retribution.

Most modes of avoidance protest are rooted in everyday peasant patterns of work, social action and even amusement. They overlap with, and are therefore often difficult to distinguish analytically from, other peasant strategies for survival such as crime, collusion with patrons or government officials, or various forms of confrontational protest, both violent and non-violent. In order to be meaningfully classified as protest, however, each mode of avoidance response must involve a conscious and articulated intent to deny resources or services or do injury to those who are perceived as the sources of their suffering, while minimising or altogether evading direct clashes with their adversaries.

THE PROTEST OF DENIAL I: EVERYDAY PEASANT RESISTANCE FROM WITHIN

By far the most difficult type of avoidance protest to study is also that which is the most pervasive. In fact, everyday forms of peasant resistance frequently straddle the nebulous zone between ongoing peasant defences and protest to such a degree that it is difficult, and perhaps unnecessary, to distinguish sharply between them. Everyday or footdragging resistance typically in-volves individual rather than collective action; it is normally aimed at specific demands rather than grand reforms; and in most instances it involves calculated errors or incompetence rather than sustained protest efforts. The aggrieved party seeks to deny labour or produce to those who are viewed as exploiters, although curses or malicious gossip represent perhaps the minimal forms of this type of protest. Everyday resistance is by definition localised and endemic to particular agrarian systems. It plays an integral role in the ongoing exchanges between elite and cultivating groups at different levels. It is characteristically so pervasive and specific that it has rarely been recorded and, until recent decades, almost never been described in detail. Indeed, our awareness of these forms of peasant response has resulted to a large degree from contemporary village studies. We have of necessity interpolated patterns of everyday protest from recent fieldwork by gleaning the bits of historical information available, borrowing heavily from studies of non-peasant societies where evidence of footdragging and cheating is more abundant [*Genovese*, 1972: 285–324, 599–657], and ultimately resorting to a good many inferences based on circumstantial evidence.

For the pre-colonial era, the only forms of everyday resistance through denial that we can discuss with any degree of certainty are collusion and concealment. Even so, we must approach these indirectly through a more general analysis of state structures and revenue collection patterns. The often substantial difference between the tribute that South or South-east Asian rulers claimed as their fair share and the amount of revenue that actually reached their coffers or labour that was actually performed in their fields or workshops provides vivid testimony of the degree to which concealment and cheating were endemic in these states. Collusion, deception and denial, however, were found at all levels from the village to the royal palace. Thus, it is difficult to know how much cultivators of different standings from landholders to landless labourers benefited from the weak communications and low level of bureaucratic organisation and commitment that made these practices so widespread and effective. It is probable that the greatest advantages derived from the denial of revenue and labour to the state went to those of highest position and power and that the returns diminished as the contest for control of scarce resources descended the social scale. Above the village level, these gains would primarily benefit the families and clients of local lords. However, the villages in many areas of South and South-east Asia were assessed and paid their taxes on a communal basis. This meant that even the most vulnerable cultivators, landless labourers, received some protection through collusion and concealment as long as they were attached to patron notables. Recent superb studies, such as those by Moertono [1968] and Lieberman [1984], have illuminated the various devices by which villagers collaborated, often with local officials, to bury harvested crops, under-report the amount of village land under cultivation, overestimate crop losses due to flooding or drought, or relocate young men in the forest when government recruiting parties were in the vicinity. Although it is highly probable that smaller-scale concealment in the form of pilfering and petty hoarding occurred on an individual basis, as yet little evidence has been uncovered to empirically validate this assumption.

Despite the fact that pre-colonial sources rarely mention them, it is reasonable to assume that other forms of everyday resistance – feigned incompetence, calculated mishaps, gestures of anger or contempt, etc. – were widespread in South and South-east Asia. In the colonial period, information on these forms of protest through denial, as well as colusion and concealment, becomes more abundant, although still thin relative to data on other types of avoidance protest. As bureaucratic control grew tighter (although not nearly as tight as was once assumed); population growth reversed population-to-land ratios once favourable to the peasantry; and European military preponderance made banditry or violent risings ever more dangerous, everyday resistance may well have increased greatly in importance.

Although highly variable in coverage and accuracy [*Dewey*, 1979], colonial revenue records make it possible for us to estimate with some degree of precision the amount of revenue lost to the government through collusion, concealment and under-reporting. These estimates in turn can give a fairly accurate picture of the nature and extent of these practices in different societies and regions under colonial rule. Special inquests into official 'corruption', such as that which forms the basis for Frykenberg's detailed study of Indian influence in the British colonial administration [*1965*], also make it possible to study in some depth the techniques and circumstances that enabled local officials and villagers to deny colonial regimes substantial sums of revenue. However, the extent to which under-reporting or cheating on tribute payments represented corruption for individual gain, as opposed to resistance to demands that were perceived to be excessive, is difficult to determine. Because colonial taxes were often levied on individual house-holds, the elements of community co-operation and (very unequally) shared benefits which characterised pre-colonial concealment devices tended to be diminished. Those who suffered the most from the erosion of village and patron–client collusion were the growing numbers of landless labourers who were perhaps the hardest hit (in proportion to their meagre incomes) by regressive head taxes or levies on salt and other essential items that were standard sources of colonial revenue.

The topics of concern and the detail of reporting found in the colonial police and revenue records and political correspondence from local officials make it possible for us to study more than collusion and concealment among everyday forms of protest. Feigned incompetence or ignorance – the very essence of footdragging protest – is reflected, for example, in innumerable revenue officials' complaints about peasant indolence or carelessness; their 'reactionary' stubborness in refusing to adopt new crops or implements; and their suspicion of, and open hostility to, public works projects, campaigns for improved village sanitation and hygiene and census taking. One of the more revealing expressions of peasant mistrust of these sorts of measures was a handbill issued by the anti-separationists in Burma in the 1920s. The flyer warned that if Burma became a Crown Colony (as the separationists wanted), no prostitutes would be allowed, every house would have to have a lavatory and it would be inspected three times a day, only government-approved water could be drunk, and the meat of animals which had died of old age or disease could not be eaten [*Christian*, 1942: 332–3].

In times of heightened social tension and conflict, such as the decade after the First World War in India, fairly abundant evidence about everyday forms of agrarian protest is available. Cultivators' refusals to work the lands of European or Indian estate-owners, peasant rejection of demands that they grow certain crops or that their plough teams be used to work estate lands, their illegal and surreptitious use of landlords' fields to pasture their cattle or plant subsistence crops, and their outright refusals to co-operate with tax or rent collectors are all recorded in considerable detail.[5] In Burma in roughly the same period, hardpressed tenants resorted to very different measures to counter landlord power and demands. Pilfering, surreptitious harvests and absconding with crops produced on landlords' fields were widespread. Some tenants took crop loans from both landlords and money-lenders and then made off with the cash they had received after working the fields they had rented for only a week or two [*Burma, RAP*, 8633, 1911: 178; *Couper*, 1924: 21; *Tin Gyi*, 1926: 11–12]. Recent oral research among cultivators who had been subjected to Portuguese cotton tribute demands during the last decades of colonial rule in Mozambique reveals the wide-spread adoption of additional forms of everyday protest. The adulteration of cotton shipped to government warehouses, the cooking of cotton seeds before planting in order to convince government officials that certain areas were unsuitable for cotton cultivation, the clandestine cultivation of food crops on fields designated for cotton, late planting, and laxity about weeding cotton fields were among the techniques adopted to frustrate Portuguese tribute demands [*Isaacman*, 1980].

Because it has often been the response of individuals or small groups, usually clandestine and localised, everyday resistance involves ideology only minimally and represents a very constricted state of peasant consciousness. Although concealment or feigned incompetence express, in a rather rudi-mentary form, core peasant convictions that, for example, the cultivation of subsistence crops should take precedence over market production, various forms of everyday resistance have tended to be more defensive and remedial than expressions of conscious and clearly articulated protest. Footdragging tactics are integral parts of the Hobbesian struggle between elites and cultivators that has been central to both pre-colonial and colonial political economies in South and South-east Asia, as in virtually all pre-industrial societies. All parties to elite–peasant exchanges have been aware of con-cealment, feigned ignorance and deception; members of elite groups habi-tually assume that peasants will resort to these measures to buffer tax and rental demands. Because they have been so individualised, so embedded in pre-colonial and colonial systems of social control, everyday forms of the protest of denial have rarely provided, if ever, a suitable basis for collective protest, even though the cumulative effects of production sabotage or crop concealment can be seen as modes of collective response. Except in situations of extreme social dislocation and political breakdown, everyday resistance is the peasants' preferred means of defence and protest. It is effective, how-ever, only in situations where political institutions and social structures remain viable. Conditions of social and political deterioration and severe economic scarcity force peasants to turn to more radical, and risky, mea-sures to protect their interests, and often, merely to survive.

THE PROTEST OF DENIAL II: EXIT

Of the many forms of avoidance protest, the most disruptive and, largely for that reason, the best documented, are those that involve the denial of labour or resources as a result of individual and collective decisions to quit positions that are no longer considered tenable or abandon particular social systems altogether. The chronic scarcity of labour and the availability of large amounts of arable, unoccupied land in pre-colonial South and South-east Asia led to continuous contests among elite groups at various levels for manpower control. This rivalry in turn provided cultivating groups with institutionalised checks on elite excesses and effective means of protest. Because these contests and potential modes of peasant resistance were so central to the dynamics of statebuilding and power maintenance in indigenous South and South-east Asian states, they are perhaps the best documented of all forms of peasant resistance in the pre-colonial era, including those involving mass peasant violence. Four main forms of the protest of denial through exit can be identified from the available sources: (1) the transfer within existing social and state systems of services from one lord to another or from nobles (including the ruler) to religious institutions; (2) flight, often *en masse*, to unoccupied areas beyond the state's control; (3) the abandonment of routine agrarian tasks in favour of membership in sectarian communities; and (4) the rejection of peasant status altogether in order to join a bandit gang or theatre troupe, enter the domestic service of a powerful lord, or become a porter or urban labourer.

Because the second form of avoidance protest by denial through exit, flight, was the most likely to be collective and hence the most disruptive of regular production routines and social control networks, it is perhaps the form of pre-colonial peasant resistance that we know the most about. It is also the form of avoidance response in which protest can be the most clearly distinguished from purely defensive measures on the one hand and the pursuit of personal advantage on the other. Although peasants migrated by individual households or whole villages to find food in times of flood or drought, to escape the depredations of warring armies, or to settle more fertile areas, abundant evidence exists that indicates that migration was also a major means of protest. Royal proclamations and bureaucratic regulations from numerous societies make it clear that large-scale peasant migrations were often regarded as signs of misrule and peasant discontent. In Thailand, for example, the migration of peasants or townsmen was linked to the very meaning of the term 'oppression'. Royal officials were ordered to ascertain whether migrant groups had in fact been oppressed and, if so, report those responsible to the king or his ministers who regarded these abuses as criminal acts [*Rabibhadana*, 1969: 73–4]. It is clear that the threat of migration gave client peasants substantial leverage in their dealings with elite patrons throughout most of South and South-east Asia.

The other form of protest through exit that is well documented for the pre-colonial era centred on the transfer of a cultivator's services from one patron to another. In working with the sources available for this sort of response, however, it is more difficult than in the case of migration to distinguish actions taken out of a desire for personal advancement from those taken to protest abuses. Frequently the two motives were intertwined, but the practice of shifting patrons was apparently so common in some pre-colonial societies that customary procedures developed by which a peasant client notified his lord of his decision to transfer his services to another patron and – in Java at least [*Carey*, 1987, Ch. 2] – provided symbolic recompense in the form of material gifts. That personal advantage was a common cause for elite transfer cannot be doubted, as the following stylised request for acceptance by a patron employed by the Ankole of East Africa makes dramatically clear:

> Give me milk; make me rich;
> keep me in mind; be my father;
> I will be your child [*Mair*, 1966: 169].

The problems of distinguishing protest expression from opportunity seeking is compounded by the fact that individual acts of client transfer are rarely recorded and never (in so far as I am aware) recounted from the viewpoint of the client. Evidence provided by Habib [1963], Onghokham [1975], Lieberman [1984], Moertono [1968] and others, however, leaves no doubt that client transfer was a major form of avoidance protest. As in the case of peasant migration, labour services (and thus potential material support) were denied in situations where obligations to royal patrons had become overly burdensome relative to that for individual nobles or religious establishments. This pattern was also followed in instances where patrons had proven incapable of protecting their clients from excessive state demands [*Onghokham*. 1975: 44]. Even though clients' decisions to transfer their services were normally made on an individual household basis, they could do considerable harm to the reputation and material base of power of the abandoned patron, particularly if other clients became convinced that the lord or notable had lost his aura of authority (*wahju, pon*, etc.) and promise of continued success [*Hanks*, 1962]. As Lieberman [1984] and Aung Thwin [1976] have convincingly shown, the cumulative effects of individual and small group client defection could mortally wound the strongest of pre-colonial states.

The existence of sectarian movements in pre-colonial South and South-east Asia is, of course, well documented. Mysticism, millenarianism, guru–chela attachments and sectarian communities were prominent, at times central, features of pre-colonial societies. Surviving sources have told us a good deal about the beliefs, organisation and activities of these communities, as well as their relations with more 'orthodox' religious leaders, local notables and pre-colonial states [*Tai*, 1983; *Mendelson*, 1975; *Ahmad*, 1964; *Eaton*, 1977]. What is virtually impossible to determine and yet crucial to the identification of avoidance protest, is the degree to which these sects as movements or the decisions of individual members to join represented acts of protest, expressions of philosophical and religious conviction, calculations of personal advantage, or a combination of all three. Even though peasant participation in these movements has been documented, we know little in detail about the composition of their adherents or how this changed over time. None the less, chronicles of dynastic decline and the pattern of sectarian recruitment and behaviour suggest that there were important connections between misrule, popular unrest and millenarian prophesies in the pre-colonial period. Because many sectarian movements stressed passive withdrawal from the wider society and the severance of ties to the existing state, they can be seen as expressions of the protest of denial through exit.

Although some evidence relating to bandit activities in the pre-colonial period has been uncovered, this form of peasant response falls more properly into the third category of avoidance discussed below, clandestine retribution, if indeed it can be classified as avoidance protest at all. Nevertheless, the initial acts of peasants who opt for banditry as a means of resistance to oppression involve flight and the denial of labour and potential productivity to members of elite groups. Unfortunately, because we have virtually no information as to why individuals in the pre-colonial period became bandits, excepting those who inherited this calling from their fathers or other relatives and were trained in much the same way a craftsman learned his trade, it is impossible to know the extent to which decisions to run away and join a bandit gang were acts of protest. This is a different question from that which has proven such a source of contention between Blok and Hobsbawm [1972], focusing on the degree to which bandits were social advocates for and defenders of exploited social groups like peasants, or simply criminals out for personal gain. It is based on the premise that an individual's decision to become a bandit may be a different form of protest than that adopted in his subsequent career, or that one may be an act of protest and not the other.

All of the major forms of protest of denial through exit persisted into the colonial period. As improved communications, an awesome advantage in military strength, and more and better trained administrators give the colonisers and their indigenous allies an ever greater preponderance of power and control over the peoples of South and South-east Asia, the various forms of avoidance protest through exit were altered in major ways and, in some cases, utterly transformed.

For decades after the imposition of colonial rule in most areas, flight remained a major response of disgruntled peasants. Large tracts of unoccupied land were still available and the European overlords found themselves heavily dependent on highly porous indigenous systems of social control. In addition, new places of refuge were added as more carefully defined boundries and territorial jurisdictions were established both within colonies and between colonial possessions and the lands of rump indigenous princedoms that survived on the fringes of most colonised areas. As new market demands and incentives multiplied, however, and European policy-makers actively sought to stimulate the settlement and cultivation of new areas that had previously been underpopulated and poorly developed, migrations became increasingly oriented to opportunity, even on the part of hardpressed, landless cultivators, and diminished as an effective mode of protest for most peasants. Population growth combined with the settlement of more accessible frontier tracts reduced the potential areas to which peasants might flee, while colonial regimes improved their capacity to monitor peasant movements and to catch and punish those who sought to escape corvée labour or revenue demands through flight. Despite these trends, migration *en masse* remained a viable peasant defence and protest option for peasants on the edges of heavily forested areas or those living in regions bordering on territory belonging to rival colonial powers or indigenous princes [*Asiwaju*, 1976; *Henningham*, 1979]. To a limited degree, migration was also adopted as a protest response by Indian nationalist leaders who encouraged peasants to abandon their villages rather than submit to British revenue demands that the nationalists had made the focal issue in their anti-colonial campaigns [*Pandey*, 1978: 173].

At the same time that protest migration diminished as a viable response for most colonised peasants, the transfer of client services also lost much of its former meaning and effectiveness. Under colonial rule contractual, cash nexus relationships increasingly supplemented or supplanted the personalist, quasi-reciprocal patron–client exchanges that had dominated pre-colonial political economies. Although patron–client links persisted in many areas changing political and socio-economic conditions and most especially population growth that resulted in population-to-land ratios that were decidedly unfavourable to cultivators at all levels, rendered these ties increasingly advantageous for patron landholders, often to the point where they could exploit and humiliate 'client' tenants or labourers with impunity [*Scott*, 1972b]. Consequently, a client's decision to transfer his services to a new employer, rather than an alternative patron, gradually became a matter of market calculation and virtually disappeared as a mode of protest. As labour was transformed from personal dependency into a depersonalised commodity, especially in the case of land– and villageless workers, it became less and less possible for the weak to use the denial of labour services as a weapon against landlord adversaries. On the contrary, the oversupply of labour in most colonised areas gave those who controlled capital and land overwhelming advantages in their everyday dealings with labour over how to apportion the increasingly scarce resources available. From lords competing, and at times clashing violently, for control of scarce manpower in the pre-colonial era, the situation had been utterly transformed into one in which increasingly impoverished tenants and labourers vied for a proportionately decreasing number of jobs.

It is probable that sectarian movements increased considerably in number and size in the colonial period in response to the imposition of 'infidel' rule and social and economic dislocations [*Tai*, 1983; *Kartodirdjo*, 1972]. Although the often substantial accounts of these movements by colonial officials need to be read with great caution due to the Europeans' (often well-founded) paranoia regarding sectarian activities and their lack of understanding with or sympathy towards the socio-cultural contexts in which these movements arose, elements of hostility towards colonial regimes and their discredited collabateur allies are often unmistakable. As studies of these movements have shown [*Drewes*, passim; *Benda* and *Castles*, 1969; *Sturtevant*, 1976: 94–5, 110–11, 176], however, the adherents of these sects often intended to register their dissent through passive withdrawal, and thus the themes of denial and exit persisted in the colonial period. These intentions were often frustrated by overly zealous cult members or the insistence of European or indigenous officials that passive sectarian movements posed threats to the colonial order. Preemptive arrests or other repressive measures were often attempted that put an end to the sect's activities or drove its adherents to violent clashes with those in power [*Holt*, 1958: 54–8; Adas, 1979: 122–30]. Thus, the protest of denial through exit was transformed into violent peasant riots or rebellion.

A peasant's decision to leave his village and join a bandit gang involved much greater risks in the colonial period than earlier times, due to many of the same changes that had transformed other modes of avoidance protest. Forest refuges were cleared and settled or regularly patrolled; police and military forces were larger and better trained and armed. They were also less likely to collude with bandit leaders and conversely more committed than pre-colonial officials to hunting down those who threatened property or the peace and order that were so treasured by colonial officials. Banditry remained an exit option in some areas [*Berque*, 1972: 127–36; *Isaacman*, 1977; *Meijer*, 1949–50], but, despite romantic legends of outlaw resistance, one that was more and more likely to lead to a life of harassment and flight, and very often a violent death.

The protest of denial through exit has never been undertaken lightly. All of its forms involve the abandonment of homes, villages, grave sites and fields that represent years, often generations, of hard work, personal commitments, and associations with kin and community. All of its forms expose those who adopt them to great risks of physical harm during their passage to new lands, patrons or communities where they hope to find a better life. Of all of the types of avoidance protest, denial through exit requires the greatest preparation, the strongest commitment, and the most pronounced break with the peasant's past life. Because many of its forms also involve collective decisions and action, from small groups of young men who set off to join a bandit gang to entire village communities which flee to escape rapacious officials, the protest of denial through exit also demands a higher level of group consciousness and ongoing commitment than other types of avoidance protest. Excepting the transfer of client services, which as noted above had much in common with everyday forms of denial protest, all forms of protest through exit force those who participate in them outside the existing socio-political system. However, the calculations, risks and common commitments of denial protest through exit create only a very constricted sense of identity that is vertically orientated to group leaders and bounded by the migrant band, sect or bandit gang. Dissident organisation remains rudimentary; group goals are narrow, remedial and specific.

Although sectarian movements can coalesce around leaders with broad visions and radical aspirations, as well as a deep-seated sense of group identity and commitment, they have rarely achieved the scale that might allow them to force major reforms in or pose as viable alternatives to pre-colonial or colonial regimes. Peasant migrants, bandits and sect members have been able in some instances to win concessions from elite adversaries or enjoy brief periods of freedom from taxes or corvée labour, but they have been ultimately repressed or recaptured by the state and social systems which they fled. Co-option, violent assault or the extension of state control into newly settled areas have invariably cut short episodes of the protest of denial through exit. Thus, forms of avoidance protest involving denial through exit can temporarily ameliorate the sources of peasant hardship, but they cannot force the sorts of changes that promote the long-term well-being of peasants.

THE PROTEST OF RETRIBUTION

If the clear delineation of categories of everyday protest and the protest of denial through exit is made difficult by the potential overlap between these responses and purely defensive measures taken to enhance personal op-portunity, the protest of retribution is often difficult to distinguish from modes of peasant resistance aimed at confrontation. Like confrontational protest, avoidance protest through retribution often involves violent assaults that may not be directed against the actual source of the peasants' discontent. Unlike confrontational protest, the protest of retribution is covert. Its perpetrators hope to do injury to those whom they view as their oppressors, but to avoid an open clash with their intended victims or the agents of the state that backs their adversaries. Although confrontational protest can involve numbers of peasants that vary from a handful of dissidents to millions of supporters of a revolutionary movement, the protest of retribution is usually carried out by individuals or small groups of peasants linked by kinship or personal acquaintance. Like everyday resistance and protest through exit, the protest of retribution is a weapon of the weak. It poses, however, a more direct threat to those who are in power and is a good deal more dangerous than most forms of the protest of denial. Although peasants who adopt any form of avoidance protest seek to prevent overt clashes with bureaucratic or landed adversaries, those who engage in the protest of retribution run the highest risk of provoking violent repressive measures.

Although the most prevalent forms of the protest of retribution – arson, vandalism, crop destruction and bandit raids – are rarely recorded in pre-colonial records, it is reasonable to infer that they were widely employed. Based on the experience of other societies where evidence is available [*Berque*, 1972; *Le Roy Ladurie*, 1974; *Thompson*, 1972], it is also probable that community modes of reprisal such as shaming, ridicule, cursing and the use of sorcery against powerful individuals who violated customary checks and ignored reciprocal obligations were employed by peasant groups throughout South and South-east Asia[6] we know, for example, that criticism of unpopular leaders frequently found its way into folk stories and songs, and especially into the splendid dance drama performances that exemplify so well the cultural ideals and worldview of South and South-east Asian peoples. As Margaret Kartoni [*1976*] has shown in her detailed analysis of the popular *reyog* dance drama of the Ponogoro region in central Java, songs and plays can be used to mock the arrogance of powerful figures, including kings. Through drama deep-seated resentment of the *priyayi* elite is also given voice through the transformation of characters who ought to be refined or *alus* into coarse, vulgar bullies. At the same time, peasant values and '*kasar* earthiness' can be affirmed.

In the colonial period, incidents of the protest of reprisal are more readily documented. Arson – the burning of crops, toll stations, estate houses or factories, and government records depots – is widely recorded in many areas of India, Java and Burma. In times of crisis widespread arson often served as the prelude to open peasant rebellion, as in the case of the burning of Chinese toll stations in Yogyakarta at the start of the Java War [*Louw* and *Klerck*, 1894, 267–73]. Clandestine incendiary attacks were also combined with non-violent forms of confrontational protest such as mass meetings and petition campaigns in areas like Bihar during the Champaran disturbances of the early 1920s to serve notice to colonial officials and nationalist leaders alike of the depth of peasant dissatisfaction and their determination to force reforms [*Henningham*, 1976: 62; *Misra*, 1963: 116, 121, 138, 140, 152]. Cases of peasant vandalism – the calculated destruction of buildings, tools, livestock, and crops – are also widely documented for the colonial period. Of particular concern to colonial authorities were acts of vandalism aimed at railways and telegraph lines that European officials rightly perceived as vital to the maintenance of colonial control [*Gillion*, 1971: 142; *Harcourt*, 1977: 319–20].

The problems of distinguishing between crime and protest identified for the pre-colonial period remain for the colonial era due to the sketchiness of most police reports on matters relating to motivation and the colonisers' penchant for labelling all manner of disturbances illegal. Even colonial officials were forced on occasion to concede, however, that robberies and assaults on landlord and moneylending groups were peasant retribution for what were perceived as exploitative practices on the part of key agents and allies of the European colonisers [*Adas*, 1982, 159ff]. Although it is a fictionalised account, Thein Pe Myint's 1934 short story, 'Her Husband or Her Money', vividly captures one instance of the protest of retribution through crime. Having killed the miserly moneylender, Me Sein, the dacoit, Kan Htaik, removes his disguise and reveals his true identity to her husband and his uncle, U Kyauk Lon. U Kyauk Lon gasps in astonishment: 'So it's you, my nephew! How could you have done such a thing?' Kan Htaik's reply epitomises the sorts of causes that drove peasants to the protest of retribution, just as his actions, clandestine and aimed at a familiar and specific target, typify this form of avoidance response:

If it had been anyone else, I wouldn't have, Uncle. I did it because I simply couldn't stand that wife of yours. All I know is that I was poor because of her. I was nearly starving, but she never gave me a helping hand. You never realised how much we contributed to her riches, did you? I don't want to talk about it. She was a mean bitch [1973: 34].

As I have argued above, banditry remained an important peasant response to oppression or opportunity throughout the colonial era. Very often bandit gangs targeted rich, but unpopular, individuals or groups that the peasantry of a given area found especially exploitative. The Chettiars in Burma, the Chinese in Java, the *vanis* of western India were favourite targets of bandit gangs during times of relative peace and the object of mob assaults in periods of crisis and social unrest [*Kumar*, 1968: Ch.5; *Adas*, 1982: 96–8]. The degree to which bandits selected moneylenders or landlords as targets because they were vulnerable and lucrative or to avenge their harsh treatment of cultivating groups varied widely from one instance to the next and is difficult to determine in most cases. A blend of both motives may have been present on many occasions, even though colonial records tend to stress the pursuit of individual gain as the cause of criminal acts.

As overt, especially violent, protest grew more dangerous, retribution through clandestine criminal acts may have increased in importance as a response of dissident peasants. Individual, small-scale robberies and assaults were less likely to be intensely investigated and punished than ongoing bandit operations which were seen by the colonial authorities as potential political threats. It was easier for those involved in specific acts of retributive protest to return to their everyday roles as peasants and law-abiding community members than was the case for full-time, professional bandits. 'Part-time' avengers were also less likely to be compelled to attack peasant communities for the means to survive, which appears to have been the case with hard-pressed dacoit gangs [*Vitalis*, 1851: 7–9; *RPAB*, 1913: 18; 1918: 17, 19]. The former were thus more likely than full-time bandits to be accepted, supported and protected by villagers who could take vicarious satisfaction in the humiliation, and even the bodily harm done to, tight-fisted moneylenders or unyielding landlords. 'Social' banditry, therefore, may have been more likely to be a part-time, or even one-shot, activity than a full-time career which is the sense in which Hobsbawm [1959, 1969] usually applies the term.

As regional elite groups and local estate owners grew more reliant on the backing of the European colonisers and more prone to live in urban areas, the power of inter-community sanctions like shaming and sorcery inevitably declined. The frequency of criminal assaults on landlords and moneylenders may indicate that stronger measures of retribution – poisoning, physical aggression, arson – became more common, but the available sources and the paucity of information the pre-colonial period, make it difficult to verify these trends. One form of the protest of retribution that almost certainly became more widespread in the colonial era was mockery. In a wide variety of forms, from gestures of contempt like the sneers Raden Adjeng Kartini observed on the faces of Javanese commoners who hastened to make way for a pompous Dutch official parading under a gold umbrella [1964: 60], to a great proliferation of vernacular pamphlets, stories, cartoons, sayings and plays, ridicule grew in importance in the colonial period as a vehicle of avoidance protest. The following description by James Peacock of a scene from a popular Javanese play performed in Surabaya illustrates the range of issues that could be captured in popular entertainments:

> A fat Dutchman appears, with much bold braid and other decorations on his uniform, blustering out pompous gutteral instructions in Indonesian to Amat. He waits for Amat to answer. Amat utters a crude Surabaya Javanese word (laughter). The Dutchman is infuriated. He gives Amat some more orders but Amat suddenly gives his shoulder a comradely shove (great laughter). The Dutchman is further enraged. Amat leaps away, smiles tensely. Now the Dutchman commands Amat to bring in the prisoners. He does so acting tough (incongruously so, since he is puny in appearance and ordinarily passive in manner); he makes them kneel to him, rattles his gun at them. The Dutchman bustles up, pats Amat on the shoulder. 'Ah yes,' he says, 'That is good. You must show your power' [1967: 48].

The coarse and insensitive Dutch bureaucrat, his puny and posturing Javanese lackey, the empty pomp, the uneasy relationship between coloniser and indigenous ally, the importance of a show of physical power are all captured in a very few words and meaningful gestures. Although the plays that Peacock describes were produced in the post-independence period, similar treatment of many of these same themes must have delighted Javanese audiences throughout the colonial era. As Peacock's summaries indicate, not only the Dutch were subjected to ridicule through popular drama. Pretentious *modins* (mosque officials who call the faithful to prayer) and corrupt and hypocritical *hadjis* are also caricatured and exposed [56]. The cultural distance that separated the Europeans from their subjects would have rendered the colonisers oblivious to most gestures of contempt or other forms of popular satire, but their indigenous allies could not have remained unaware of the bitter criticism and perhaps the implicit threats expressed by the characters and themes portrayed by travelling dance and drama performers. Detailed study may well show that these performances were major means of arousing anti-colonial sentiments and mobilising the peasantry for struggles aimed at achieving independence throughout South and South-east Asia.

Excepting ridicule through songs and plays, the protest of retribution involves perhaps the least developed consciousness of the three main types of avoidance protest. Although there is the satisfaction of revenge, of being able to injure their enemies, peasants, acting in small groups, engage in acts of retribution that are clandestine, transitory and aimed at individual material or human targets. Thus, most forms of the protest of retribution represent very limited responses that flaunt laws and threaten individuals, but have little lasting impact on existing systems of peasant–elite exchange and social control. This is not true, however, of ridicule through popular arts and entertainments which reaches the widest audience, is the most generalised of the forms of the protest of retribution in terms of targets, and is a potent means of articulating peasant grievances and more fundamental ethical values. Not surprisingly, of all of the forms of avoidance protest, ridicule in its various guises has been the most readily harnessed to more broadly based, more ideologically sophisticated peasant protest movements, both nationalist/anticolonial and Marxist/revolutionary [*Ngo Vinh Long*, 1973; *Anderson*, 1965, 1966].

BEYOND AVOIDANCE PROTEST

It is difficult to know with any certainty the degree to which avoidance protest in its many forms either obviated against or served as a prelude to more aggressive, better organised modes of peasant resistance involving direct confrontations with those who are viewed as oppressors. It is probable that the nature of these connections varies by the general type and particular form in question. Forms of everday protest through denial are likely to prevent the adoption of more radical measures as long as they provide effective defences for cultivating groups and, concomitantly, the systems of exchange and control in which they are employed remain viable. Severe social dislocations or sudden increases in the power of elite groups that allow them to override customary restraints and peasant buffers can force cultivators to turn to other types of avoidance protest – exit or retribution – which are less embedded in existing institutions or to modes of overt confrontation from petition processions to jacqueries.

Even though most forms of the protest of denial through exit place aggrieved peasants outside existing state systems and elite/peasant exchange networks at least temporarily, they are unlikely to bring about solutions to the underlying causes of agrarian unrest. Flawed political economies are abandoned rather than reformed or overthrown and reconstituted. In fact, because forms of denial protest through exit are orientated to evasion, they often have effects that act against amelioration of the conditions that lead to peasant unrest. They release pent-up anger and disperse those who are disgruntled, at times rendering them more vulnerable to reprisals by their elite adversaries. In the case of client transfer or individual flight, protest through exit may dampen mounting collective discontent by drawing highly conscious and vocal individuals out of situations of frustration and humiliation and offering them alternative, and potentially more rewarding, careers.

It is difficult to document convincingly, but there is some evidence that cultivators who engage in the protest of retribution are those most likely to become involved in direct confrontations with elite adversaries. Police reports, special enquiries into peasant risings and related sources indicate that a high proportion of peasants who join in mass demonstrations, riots or rebellions had previously been convicted of acts which those in power labelled 'crimes'. It may be that agriculturists who are willing to risk capture and bodily injury while committing surreptitious acts of reprisal, are also those most willing to brave the counter-reprisals of incumbent elites who are openly challenged. However, the individual or small group orientation and the limited consciousness associated with most forms of the protest of retribution mean that recruiting and organisational skills and ideological sophistication must come from beyond poorly educated, provincially minded peasant groups who are too much caught up in daily efforts to survive to formulate grand revolutionary designs. Avoidance protest in its many forms can protect, win specific concessions or exact revenge, but it cannot reform in major ways or transform unjust socio-political systems. Only modes of confrontational protest can achieve the latter and, if the history of agrarian revolution is any guide, non-peasant, elite allies are essential to the mobilisation and success of peasant resistance once it moves beyond the protest of avoidance.

NOTES

1. 'The common or little man never complains publicly'. A peasant's response to Dutch queries as to why the migrants had not complained about worsening conditions earlier while they were still in Semarang [*Pierson*, 1868: 155].
2. For examples, see the essays in the volume on Maroon societies edited by Richard Price [1979] and the studies by Mullin [1972], Hilton [1973] and Blum [1961].
3. Including environmental factors and modes of peasant adaptation to these which Elizabeth Perry [1980] has shown may greatly influence the modes of defence and protest that peasants adopt.
4. For a fine discussion of these patterns in a very different historical and societal setting see Beqiraj [1966].
5. For examples of these forms of resistance see Government of Bihar and Orissa, *Police Proceedings*, 17 Jan. 1913, enclosure A2; Vol. 9793, 1915, No. 28, p. 3; Vol. 10291, 1918, No. 37, p. 2; Vol. 11383, 1924, No. 8, pp. 2–3. See also Pandey [1978: 172, 181]; Hardiman [1977: 56, 58ff].
6. This assumption is supported by numerous anthropological accounts based on research conducted in recent decades which relate the existence of these practices in the post-independence era.

REFERENCES

Adas, Michael, 1979, *Prophets of Rebellion: Millenarian Protest against the European Colonial Order*, Chapel Hill: University of North Carolina Press.
Adas, Michael, 1982, 'Bandits, Monks, and Pretender Kings: Patterns of Peasant Resistance and Protest in Colonial Burma, 1826–1941', in Robert P. Weller and Scott E. Guggenheim, *Power and Protest in the Countryside*, Durham, NC: Duke University Press.
Ahmad, Aziz, 1964, *Studies in Islamic Culture in the Indian Environment*, Oxford: Oxford

University Press.

Anderson, Benedict R. O'G., 1965, *Mythology and the Tolerance of the Javanese*, Ithaca, NY: Cornell University Press.

Anderson, Benedict R. O'G., 1966, 'The Languages of Indonesian Politics', *Indonesia*, Vol. 1, No. 1.

Asiwaju, A.I., 1976, 'Migrations as Revolt: The Example of the Ivory Coast and the Upper Volta before 1945', *Journal of African History*, Vol. 17, No. 4.

Aung Thwin, Michael, 1976, 'Kingship, the *Sangha* and Society in Pagan', in Kenneth Hall and J. Whitmore (eds.), *Explorations in Early Southeast Asian History: Origins of Statecraft*, Ann Arbor: University of Michigan.

Benda, Harry and Lance Castles, 1969, 'The Samin Movement', *Bijdragen tot de Taal-Land-en Volkenkunde*, Vol. 125, No. 2.

Beqiraj, Mehmet, 1966, *Peasantry in Revolution*, Ithaca, NY: Cornell University Press, 1966.

Berque, Jacques, 1972, *Egypt: Imperialism and Revolution*, New York: Praeger.

Blok, Anton, 1972, 'The Peasant and the Brigand: Social Banditry Reconsidered', *Comparative Studies in Society and History*, Vol. 14, No. 4.

Bihar and Orissa, Government of, 1913–22, *Police Proceedings*, India Office Records, London, England.

Blum, Jerome, 1961, *Lord and Peasant in Russia*, Princeton: Princeton University Press.

Bremen, Jan, 1982, 'The Village on Java and the Early Colonial State', *The Journal of Peasant Studies*, Vol. 9, No. 4.

Carey, Peter, 1987, *Pangeran Dipanagara and the Origins of the Java War, 1825–1830*, Leiden: forthcoming.

Christian, J.L., 1942, *Modern Burma*, Berkeley: University of California Press.

Couper, Thomas, 1924, *Report of Inquiry into the Condition of Agricultural Tenants and Labourers*, Rangoon: Government of Burma.

Dewey, Clive, 1979, '*Patwari* and *Chaukidar*: Subordinate Officials and the Reliability of India's Agricultural Statistics', in Clive Dewey and A.G. Hopkins (eds.), *The Imperial Impact in Africa and South Asia*, London: Institute of Commonwealth Studies.

Drewes, Gerardus W.J., 1925, *Drie Javaansche Goeroe's: Hun Leven, Onderricht en Messias-prediking*, Leiden: Vros.

Eaton, Richard, 1977, *Sufis of Bijapur, 1300–1700: Social Roles of Sufis in Medieval India*, Princeton: Princeton University Press.

Fasseur, Cornelis, 1978, *Kultuurstelsel en Koloniale Baten: De Nederlandse Exploitatie van Java 1840–1860*, Leiden: University of Leiden.

Frykenberg, Robert E., 1965, *Guntur District 1788–1848: A History of Local Influence and Central Authority in South India*, Oxford: Oxford University Press.

Genovese, Eugene, 1972, *Roll, Jordan, Roll: The World the Slaves Made*, New York: Pantheon.

Gillion, K.L., 1971, 'Gujarat in 1919', in R. Kumar (ed.), *Essays on Gandhian Politics*, Oxford: Oxford University Press.

Habib, Irfan, 1963, *The Agrarian System of Mughal India*, Aligarh: Aligarh University Press.

Hanks, Lucien, 1962, 'Merit and Power in the Thai Social Order', *American Anthropologist*, Vol. 64, No. 6.

Harcourt, Max, 1977, 'Kisan Populism and Revolution in Rural India: The 1942 Disturbances in Bihar and East United Provinces', in D. A. Low (ed.), *Congress and the Raj*, London: Heinemann.

Hardimann, David, 1977, 'The Crisis of the Lesser Patidars: Peasant Agitations in Kheda District, Gujarat, 1917–34', in Low, *Congress and Raj*.

Henningham, Stephen, 1976, 'The Social Setting at the Champaran Satyagraha: The Challenge of an Alien Elite', *Indian Economist and Social History Review*, Vol. 13, No. 3.

Henningham, Stephen, 1979, 'Agrarian Relations in North Bihar', *Indian Social and Economic History Review*, Vol. 16, No. 1.

Hilton, Rodney, 1973, *Bond Men Made Free*, New York: Viking.

Hobsbawm, Eric, 1959, *Primitive Rebels*, New York: Norton.

Hobsbawm, Eric, 1969, *Bandits*, New York: Dell.

Holt, P.M., 1958, *The Mahdist State in the Sudan 1881–1890*, Oxford: Oxford University Press.

Isaacman, Allen, 1977, 'Social Banditry in Zimbabwe (Rhodesia) and Mozambique, 1894–1907: An Expression of Early Peasant Protest', *Journal of Southern African Studies*, Vol. 4, No. 1.

Isaacman, Allen, Stephen, Michael, *et al.*, 1980, ' "Cotton is the Mother of Poverty": Peasant Resistance to Forced Cotton Production in Mozambique, 1938–1961', *International Journal of African Studies*, Vol. 13, No. 4.

Kartini, Raden Adjeng, 1964, *Letters of a Javanese Princess*, New York: Norton.

Kartodirdjo, Sartono, 1972, 'Agrarian Radicalism in Java', in Claire Holt (ed.), *Culture and Politics in Indonesia*, Ithaca, NY: Cornell University Press.

Kartoni, Margaret, 1976, 'Performance, Music and Meaning of Reyog Ponogoro', *Indonesia*, Vol. 22, No. 1.

Kumar, Ravindra, 1968, *Western India in the Nineteenth Century*, London: Routledge & Kegan Paul.

Last, Murray, 1970, 'Aspects of Administration and Dissent in Hausaland, 1800–1968', *Africa*, Vol. 40, No. 4.

Le Roy Ladurie, Emmanuel, 1974, *The Peasants of Languedoc*, Urbana: University of Illinois Press.

Liebermann, Victor, 1984, *Southeast Asian Administrative Cycles: The Burmese Pattern, c. 1590–1760*, Princeton: Princeton University Press.

Louw, Pieter and E.S. de Klerck, 1894, *De Java-Oorlog van 1825–1830*, The Hague: Nijhoff.

Mair, Lucy, 1966, *Primitive Government*, Baltimore: Penguin.

Meijer, D.H., 1949–50, 'Over het bendwezen op Java', *Indonesië*, Vol. 3, No. 2.

Mendelson, E. Michael, 1975, *State and Sangha in Burma*, Ithaca, NY: Cornell University Press.

Moertono, Soemarsaid, 1968, *State and Statecraft in Old Java*, Ithaca, NY: Cornell University Press.

Mullin, Gerald W., 1972, *Flight and Rebellion: Slave Resistance in Eighteenth-Century Virginia*, Oxford: Oxford University Press.

Ngo Vinh Long, 1973, *Before the Revolution: The Vietnamese Peasants under the French*, Cambridge, MA: MIT Press.

Onghokham, 1975, 'The Residency of Madium Pryayi and Peasant in the Nineteenth Century', Ph. D. dissertation, Yale University.

Pandey, Gyanendra, 1978, *The Ascendancy of the Congress in Uttar Pradesh, 1926–34*, New Delhi: Oxford University Press.

Peacock, James, 1967, 'Anti-Dutch, Anti-Muslim Drama among Surabaya Proletarians: A Description of Performances and Responses', *Indonesia*, Vol. 4, No. 1.

Perry, Elizabeth, 1980, *Rebels and Revolutionaries in North China, 1845–1945*, Palo Alto, CA: Stanford University Press.

Pierson, N.G., 1868, *Het Kultuurstelsel: Zes Voorlezingen*, Amsterdam: Van Kampen.

Price, Richard (ed.), 1979, *Maroon Societies: Rebel Slave Communities in the Americas*, Baltimore: Johns Hopkins University Press.

RAP, 1911, Government of Burma, *Revenue and Agriculture Proceedings*, India Office Records: London, England.

Rabibhadana, Akin, 1969, *The Organization of Thai Society in the Early Bangkok Period*, Ithaca, NY: Cornell University Press.

RPAB, 1911–1919, Government of Burma, *Report(s) on the Police Administration of Burma*, London: India Office Records.

Scott, James, 1972a, 'Patron–Client Politics and Political Change in Southeast Asia', *American Political Science Quarterly*, Vol. 66, No. 1.

Scott, James, 1972b, 'The Erosion of Patron–Client Bonds and Social Change in Southeast Asia', *The Journal of Asian Studies*, Vol. 22, No. 1.

Scott, James and Kerkvliet, Ben, 1973, 'The Politics of Survival: Peasant Responses to "Progress" in Southeast Asia', *Journal of Southeast Asian Studies*, Vol. 4, No. 2.

Soest, G.H. van, 1869, *Geschiedenis van het Kultuurstelsel*, Rotterdam: H. Nijgh.

Sturtevant, David R., 1976, *Popular Uprisings in the Philippines*, Ithaca, NY: Cornell University Press.

Tai, Hue-Tam Ho, 1983, *Millenarianism and Peasant Politics in Vietnam*, Cambridge, MA: Harvard University Press.

Than Tun, 1968, 'Administration of King Tha-lun (1629–48)', *Journal of the Burma Research Society*, Vol. 51, No. 2.

Thein Pe Myint, 1973, 'Her Husband or Her Money', in P.M. Milne (trans.), *Selected Short Stories of Thein Pe Myint*, Ithaca, NY: Cornell University Press.

Thompson, Edward, 1972, '"Rough Music": Le Charivari anglais', *Annales: économies sociétés civilisations*, Vol. 27, No. 3.

Tin Gyi, U., 1926, *Myaungmya Settlement Report, 1924–25*, Rangoon: Government of Burma.

Vitalis, L., 1851, *De invoering, werking en gebreken van het stelsel van Kultuurs op Java*, Zalt-Bommel: Norman en zoon.

Tenants' Non-Violent Resistance to Landowner Claims in a Central Luzon

Brian Fegan*

THE CONTEXT OF RESISTANCE

Although this study focuses on individual non-violent everyday forms of resistance in the early 1970s when I was in a village in northern Bulacan province for two years, it is important to see these forms in historical context. Peasants in this area 80 kilometres from Manila are no strangers to collective violent confrontation with the landowners and their private forces or with the state.

Peasant movements in Central Luzon since the 1840s drew on three major ideas strands [*Fegan*, 1978; 1982: 106–12]: First was a folk-catholic idea about the 'return' of a hero identified with light and sunrise who would arise in the East to liberate the people/nation from 300 years of dark and suffering [*Ileto*, 1979]. In the 1890s folk catholics reinterpreted nationalist ideas to conceive a hero who would unite the people in a brotherhood that would redeem them from oppression by a foreign governor and his troops (identified with Pilate), allied with the native rich and the false religious leaders (identified with the scribes and pharisees who persecuted Christ). After the war with Spain, then the US from 1896–1902 peasants identified the liberator with both the national martyr Jose Rizal and with General Ricarte who refused to accept defeat but went into exile. From Hong Kong then Japan, Ricarte kept alive the idea of lower-class liberation from both the collaborating rich men of the nation, and the US colonial regime, promising that he would return with guns to lead secret patriotic brotherhoods in a general rising. From the early 1900s peasant radicals joined illegal fraternities and drilled awaiting the new dawn. There were several abortive local risings up to 1935 on this class/nationalist/millenarian line. The third strand was a kind of folk socialism, propagated among Manila workers from as early as about 1902, drawing on Marxist and anarchist ideas brought in by intellectuals returning from study abroad, and spread by radicals connected with the Printers Union. By the time of the First World War Marxist ideas of exploitation, the organisational form of unions, and collective bargaining as a tactic had spread to peasants in the provinces close to Manila. On the way they were reinterpreted through and amalgamated with the pre-existing ideas of national liberation through a rising. By the late 1920s a national

*Macquarie University, North Ryde 2113, Australia.

confederation of peasant unions was led by radicals drawn from the Printers Union and foundation members of the fledgling Communist Party. Urban Marxist intellectuals in the Depression of the 1930s had difficulty restraining peasant members from precipitating local armed risings.

In the Pacific war of the 1940s the sudden collapse of the US-backed Commonwealth government and the proximity of Pacific War battlefields to the densely populated plain, provided arms plus the absence of a legitimate state power. The peasant unions became the basis for the Hukbalajap (Peoples Anti-Japanese Army) guerrillas that, under leadership of men who were nominally members of the Communist Party, dominated the region from 1943–45. The return of US forces restored the landlord-dominated economy and political system that peasants had lived without for a couple of years. However, with arms, region-wide organisation in the PKM peasant union and top leadership by radicals who had become popular heroes in the occupation, the peasants were in a different mood and tactical situation. They had expected great gains from national independence in 1946. When, instead, they found the landlords using private armies to break the PKM peasant union and liquidate its leadership, and that the congressmen they elected were ejected from their seats, peasant unionists returned to their units and guns. The peasant war from 1946 to 1953 brought PKM-HMB guerrillas, the 'Huks' into conflict with landlord recruited and paid Civilian Guards units, with the Philippines Constabulary, and the Army [*Kerkvliet*, 1977]. The peasants suffered forced evacuation of isolated settlements, search and destroy operations, skirmishes between guerrillas and the landlord or state forces, and imposition of armed overseers to supervise the harvests. By 1953 both sides were exhausted and had learned lessons about how far they could press certain claims.

By and large, the landlords reduced their real if not their formal claims on the crop. The peasant war had been costly for them. Farms abandoned in the fighting produced no income at all. The peasants were sullen and detiant; elements of the guerrillas remained in the field. Big landowners faced a choice: on one hand they could attempt to reimpose the strict supervision of harvest through armed men on the lines of the Civilian Guard units that had helped provoke the peasant war and would cost five per cent of receipts. Alternatively, they could withdraw armed guards, allow peace to return and have tenants come back to their lands. But if the overseers were themselves peasants, then there would be a degree of under-reporting of the harvest as a result of peasant stratagems and of unarmed resident village-level overseers' need to turn a blind eye or collude. Meantime the owners resisted the conservative land reform laws introduced by US-supported President Magsaysay who had as Secretary of War reformed the army and had a large role in suppressing the rebellion. The landowner-dominated Congress watered down the laws, then ensured insufficient funds were voted to implement them [*Murray*, 1972: 157–8].

The peasants were exhausted by the war. The majority wanted to get back to farming and their families. But the withdrawal of armed estate guards, and the caution the overseers had learned in fear of provoking assassination by social bandit remnants of the rebels, allowed a covert rent reduction. In effect peasant, overseer and landlord accepted a compromise. Legally, peasants under successive paper reforms were entitled to 60 per cent or 70 per cent of the crop. In fact landowner and peasant contracted for formal 50/50 shares. But as overseers could not press beyond a reasonable limit for revelation of the full harvest, peasants got more than 50 per cent by under-declaring. There was a kind of armed truce all round, in which the parties, depending on the local balance of force, adopted circumspect behaviour. Meantime the state, partly in response to US and to urban pressure, enacted further reform laws that increased the peasant paper share, regulated terms of share tenancy, and from 1964 proposed an eventual shift to fixed rent tenancies based on 25 per cent of average net harvests.

Although the failure of the revolt had a chilling effect on overt peasant resistance it had no less effect on landowner and state perceptions of what was necessary and possible. Most of the big landowners had abandoned the rural towns to live full-time in Manila. This was in part the continuation of the pre-war pull of professional careers, urban investments and the elite social and political life of the capital, but in part fear of ambush. They left the estates in control of professional managers who had full powers to take on and discharge tenants, lend to tenants for farm expenses and subsistence, issue seed, supervise use of estate dams, pumps, tractors and threshing machines but, above all, to settle accounts with the tenants at threshing time and bring in the land's share of the crop plus credit recovered at high interest. Beneath these were village-based overseers and harvest checkers who were for the most part trusty tenants. Medium landowners based in town used trusty tenants as informal overseers but reserved control of credit to themselves. The smallest landowners supervised tenants directly. In the main, landowners' contacts with tenants were limited to issuing credit before the crop season opened, then policing the harvest in order to extract the land's share plus credit at threshing.

As it happens, several of those managers and top overseers of the 1950s and 1960s that I interviewed turned out to be ex-peasant unionists and/or rebels. These were men with a reputation for the ability to handle difficult situations, including a reputation for effective use of violence. They maintained apparently contradictory roles, representing a landowner as his overseer on an estate away from their own village, but standing up for the rights of tenants in their own village against the landowners' overseers there. They also had a sideline as ward heelers and fixers in electoral politics, guards for illegal loggers, etc. These *magaling na lalaki*, 'superlative males' are best considered as entrepreneurs in violence. A reputation for effective use of force made them sought after, like well-known lawyers, to represent one or other party in a dispute. Given the weakness of the state in rural areas, and its non-monopoly of arms, disputes tended to be settled according to the balance of effective threat of the use of force between the parties (or their representatives) rather than by reference to police and criminal law courts. The categories 'social bandit', rebel, revolutionary that writers like Hobsbawm [1965, 1969] have used for 'protectors of the poor' cannot be usefully applied to individuals occupying such contradictory roles. In this entrepreneurial style a man with a reputation may be at once protector of the poor in one village, protector of the rich in another, and in the meantime occasional predatory bandit to strangers and adept at intervening in electoral politics. The capacity to deliver votes ensured many such men a measure of immunity from the attention of the local mayor and his police. Although they had always been around, such men flourished in the unsettled times from the 1940s to the end of the 1960s. About that time professional political brokers began to replace entrepreneurs in violence. From the 1960s the state became both more powerful and richer so that allocation of pork-barrel funds through networks of candidates and brokers, and the secret ballot made less effective the methods of those *magaling na lalaki* who failed to adapt.

Meanwhile, the villages that had formerly consisted almost exclusively of tenants and smallholder peasants lost their class homogeneity. They became internally divided between households with farms and a rapidly increasing proportion of landless labourer households. This arose because the population was doubling at each generation. Under tenancy, a farm under about 2.5 hectares is not divisible among the tenant's children. It goes to only one of them as successor. The rest, if not placed at the frontier, in urban, industrial or other non-agricultural livings fall into the landless rural labourer class. Philippine industry failed to expand employment fast enough to absorb the population increase so that most of the new households stayed in the villages. Landless households could not participate in exchange labour, but needed paid work. Exchange and feast labour for most tasks collapsed in the 1940s carrying with them some of the preconditions for political cooperation. Relations between farm operator and his labour force at peak labour seasons like transplanting and harvest were reduced to money or crop-share wages. Moreover, the landless labourers were dependent on tenants for access to house lots. Villagers with farms became a privileged class in conflict with the landless over wage rates and house lots, but able to allocate scarce work, house lots and loans. The farmer households were able to create petty pyramids of patronage useful in village faction and electoral politics. Until the 1950s village and countryside were able to unite as communities of members of one class, tenants, against the landowners in the towns and city. The emergence of a new underclass threw division into the villages and cost that unity [*Fegan*, 1978, 1982].

These processes occurred within a couple of generations. It is not surprising then that old men who lived through the period of patriotic fraternities and peasant unions, the Pacific War and the Peasant War, have different perspectives from younger ones who had more years of formal education, and have been influenced by new ideas picked up in school, Manila, from their transistors and more recently, TV. Nevertheless, they are members of the same families and villages, and the culture accords great respect to seniority, while a majority of farm holders are men over 50. It is important therefore to bear in mind that the appreciation of new situations and the selection of tactics to deal with them is made or influenced by men whose view of the present is enriched and coloured by their experience of a complex past.

With the suppression of the rebellion in the early 1950s peasants returned to farming but as the PKM union had been made illegal, and they lacked a class-interest party, there were few means by which non-violent pressures might be mounted to have the land reform laws altered to give them teeth, or implemented. Nevertheless, there were non-peasant pressures on the government to respond with reform to the running sore of the agrarian problem. The United States missions had backed President Magsaysay and his reform law, enacted in 1954. The US was concerned, in the context of the cold war, the communist victory in China, and the developing conflict in Indo-China, to press for reforms that would pacify the peasantry and under-cut the appeal of rebels. Some Philippines urban liberals were reacting to new social justice strands in the Catholic Church. Presidential candidates after Magsaysay were aware of the populist potential of reform promises. A further reform law in 1963 bolstered the control of conditions of share tenancy but also allowed tenants to petition for transfer from share tenancy to fixed rent tenancy based on 25 per cent of the average net harvest. Once again the legislature allotted limited funds for implementing the reform.

From about 1969 the Jesuit-led FFF and Marxist-led Masaka peasant organisations began mounting marches to Manila and a permanent dele-gation outside the Congress. They were supported by radical Manila college students, young clergy, liberals and urban unionists. In 1971 an amendment to the reform laws declared the whole country a land reform area, legislated for compulsory fixed-rent tenancy, and beefed up the funds and imple-menting agencies. Land reform implementation was impeded in the coun-tryside by the reluctance of some tenants to cut ties with their landowners in view of the sanctions owners could bring to bear against them [*Fegan*, 1972], crucially over the matter of credit and houselots, plus the uneven struggle that a poor peasant faced in the courts.

Nevertheless the laws themselves and the prospect of their implemen-tation created conditions in which the climate of public opinion favoured the peasants. This was despite the collapse of the armed peasant movement into mafias in some areas and social bandits in others, weakening of the or-ganised peasants, and the loss of class unity in the villages and countryside. Moreover, the prospect of an eventual shift from share to fixed rent tenancy based on a proportion of average past harvests gave a further motive for peasants to wish to hold down their revealed harvests.

I now turn to the everyday forms of resistance encountered in my field village in the 1970s, a period coinciding with the early implementation of the 1971 reform, and the first impact of the 'Green Revolution'. It is worth pointing out that the researcher brings his own biases to the field. I was concerned to investigate the strategies and tactics of peasants as economic and political actors. My research focus led me to concentrate initially on the measurement of farms and the physical and labour inputs and outputs of farms and households, then as my fluency in the language improved, to find out what peasants thought they were doing. But other human factors were at work. I made close friends with some peasants, had more mutually guarded relations with those who were factional enemies of my friends, and courteous acquaintance with the majority. As it happened some of those who became friends were ex-rebels, despite a recurrent suspicion that I might be a CIA agent.

IDEOLOGIES AND MORALITIES

Throughout two years in the field I was constantly baffled by the con-tradictory ways peasants talked about the tenancy system in general or about their own relations with particular landlords. At one level this represented conflicting ideologies. One corresponded to the ideology of rent capitalism [*Fegan*, 1981], justifying the mutual dependence of labour and capital. Against this stood a counter-ideology that began from the premises of human equality, labour as the source of all wealth, and the illegitimacy of landed property and capital owned by a few who drew unearned income from the labour of the many. At a deeper level this set of contradictory propositions partly expressed a broader conflict between opposed tendencies in peasant thinking and behaviour about exchange. At one selfish pole stands pragmatic acceptance of the imperfect world at hand, within which each man must do the best he can for himself and his family, exchanging with others only to get power over them so as to constrain a geater return for himself, while eternally vigilant of the moves of others. This view would be familiar enough to Hobbes, Banfield, Sahlin's domestic mode of production Popkin, and the 'political economy' position. At the altruistic pole stands rejection of the corrupt world so that men must seek the light in order to purify their inner beings, join together as siblings, co-operate for the common good, be prepared to die to bring about a world in which men give to others without thought of return. Elements of this view would be familiar enough to Christ, Rousseau, Marx, but are an extreme statement of the 'moral economy' position. Peasants, as much as professors, are capable of posing the two views. Both tendencies are inherent in primitive exchange, as Mauss [1929] noted.

Among Central Luzon peasants the millenarian view is always present, partly because it is thrown up in everday life, in Levi-Straussian fashion, but by turning upside down not the logical but the moral features of the real world. Partly it is stated by the ideal behaviour of mythical and legendary figures like Christ, millenarian leaders of the past, and certain Huk leaders during the rebellion. The Huk of wartime and the early peasant war, whether because of their own ideals, what peasant expectations constrained them to, or what selective memory enshrines, are remembered as exemplars of the selfless behaviour of the unworldly.

That ideal behaviour is also embodied in the behaviour of local mystical curers, who (unlike doctors) heal without thought of return. Those who become curers first symbolically die or go to the mountains to leave behind human culture, family and society, then are 'reborn' bearing the power to cure individual ills. It is part of the mystique of the curer that he sets no fees, accepts whatever is freely offered to him, since to ask for payment for exercise of a power that is a free gift of the supernatural would be to lose that gift.

In the everyday, these contradictory tendencies prove able to lie side by side in the individual mind. True, some men as a matter of character play out their lives more towards one pole than the other: in normal times the general behaviour of the peasants tends towards the family-centred pole, in extraordinary times to the altruistic pole. Again, the content and tone of spontaneous conversations concerning landlords are partly set by context. Not every peasant is ready to talk freely in the presence of someone believed to be an intimate of his landlord, so that some speech was necessarily guarded or indirect. But what baffled me repeatedly was the switch, within one individual's discourse, and within a few minutes between Hobbesian pragmatism and Rousseauan idealism. Part of what is at stake resembles what games theorists have discussed as 'the free-loader problem', that is, the dilemma of moral man in a Hobbesian world. Clearly, it is irrational for an individual and irresponsible behaviour towards his own family, for him to be first to behave altruistically unless he has assurance that all others will behave similarly. In the real world this can be accommodated, as Sahlins [1974: 190–204] noted, by playing Rousseauan exchange towards family and intimates, measured reciprocity to the next circle of known partners, but Hobbesian exchange towards strangers. It is part of the reordering of values that appears with curers, millenarian movements and rebels that they cut themselves off from family, 'die' to their former selves and are reborn as 'children' of some abstraction – God, the Nation, Sweat so that they become 'sibling' to each other. In this morally exalted condition they extend familial behaviour even to strangers. Thus discourse in the ideal vein is not specifically subversive of the tenancy system. It is subversive of the whole of everyday social relations outside of the family conceived as exchanges. The uneven prior wealth and power situation, and the uneven actual exchange inherent in share tenancy are only instances of wider amoral exchange-for-advantage. Peasants do not rebel only to make landlords good. Some are prepared to die in extraordinary times to make all men good, beginning with themselves.

But in the everday of normal times, to survive they must follow the lower morality in which responsibility to family and friend take precedence over ethical recognition of the stranger. Many men talking to me privately about the stratagems they use to survive, broke off to say they found theft from the landlord, working for the landlord as guards, arms dealing, etc. distasteful. But what else could a person with children do?

The lower morality, combined with admiration for the fearless male culminates in the figure of the bandit or politico, entrepreneur in violence who protects his family and 'his own' people from political rivals, receives tribute from protegées, makes unstable coalitions or negotiates bargains with rivals, while preying selectively on strangers.

The peasants in my village were not homogeneous. A majority were landless, although some of these had fairly secure non-agricultural jobs or petty businesses. But all those who held farms were tenants, although a handful, in addition, owned or held homestead rights to third-class land outside the village. The farm-holders themselves were not pure farmers. Most had been or were engaged in non-farm self-employment or wage work, full-time or seasonally while other members of their households had diverse farm and non-farm incomes [*Fegan*, 1979].

Takahashi [1969] has argued that the share tenant in the mid-1960s diverted his labour away from the farm to seek off-farm and non-farm income sources precisely because the claims of the landlord on the crop left no incentive to increase yields. As a consequence the tenant, according to Takahashi, expended the minimum effort on his farm consistent with keeping the tenancy as one among several income sources, plus a source of credit. This form of resistance depends on there being alternative income sources and on the tenant having enough security of tenure to avoid being displaced in favour of a more diligent competitor. It may also be connected with the style of policing the harvest being such as to deter the tenant from secreting sufficient of the grain to make worthwhile a greater labour input.

Holding a farm confers more advantages than the crop share as tenant. In a totally owned landscape cut up into tenant farms only landowners or the agricultural tenants have a direct right to a houselot. On it the holder is able to grow bamboos for building material, useful trees for firewood, fruit, medicinal and minor industrial use and to raise livestock, fish and vegetables. He can also conduct backyard industries like carpentry, cart-making, vehicle repair. With relatively secure tenure he can build a house of permanent materials, concrete pig-pens, and install a tubewell for drinking water. In Central Luzon landowners have no legal or customary right to these or the grass, straw from threshing, or stubble that can be used to feed buffalo. Although they had a right in law and custom to a share of the net output of vegetables, etc. grown on rice-land out of season, and to bamboos and mangoes from the houseyard, few owners attempted to assert or police such claims. However, that the prospect of eviction from a tenancy right meant more than loss of the farm right was an additional constraint on the form and extent of tenant resistance to landowners.

Against this background of changing class relations, peasant movements and legal contexts, and despite the contradictions between higher and lower moralities, there has been one constant. At threshing time when the fruits of the season's labour, spared from typhoon, floods, diseases, insects and rats are at last safe, and the harvesters paid, they are not the farmer's. The landowner's agent is at hand with his tally sheets, his debt accounts, and a truck to cart away a large proportion of the grain. From what is left the farmer must meet his costs and other claims and support his family to next harvest. Farmers use covert stratagems in the tense harvest period to increase their short-run retained rice, and to reduce long-run claims on the harvest by landlords.

Claims on the Harvest and Stratagems to Evade Them

A tenant farmer stands to gain both immediately and in the long term from understating the harvest, so as to reduce the revealed grain against which others might press claims. Class superiors – landlord and creditor – have claims on his farm's revealed crop that will reduce what the tenant is allowed to retain from it. Class equals and inferiors – kinsmen, neighbours, landless labourers, and the village poor have claims on his household's revealed retained rice.

Evading Claims by Class Superiors

In the short term, under share tenancy the tenant stands to gain the land's share of any rice he can secretly thresh so that it does not appear in the revealed crop for division. Under lease or share tenancy, a tenant with large debts may be able to defer or default if he reveals a very low harvest, while any rice he can prevent revealing is not exposed to seizure for debt. In the long term, the prospect of a land reform like the amendment of 1971 or decree of 1972 that sets the fixed lease rent, or the purchase price of the land, in proportion to the average (revealed) normal harvest of the farm, makes it politic to keep that average low.

Landlords know that tenants have good reasons to understate the harvest – just as landowners understate the amount of land they have, its value, and their income so as to avoid taxes and land reform, while they let their land at illegal rents, charge illegally high interest on loans, and keep false books of account where principal plus interest on loans is entered as *hiram* 'a loan without interest'. Landlords employ *katiwala* overseers to police the harvest, with the object of preventing their tenants from understating.

In a tightly policed harvest on a large estate the overseers may attempt to count the sheaves in the field, take the average yield of a number of sheaves pre-threshed under supervision and try to ensure that the full count of sheaves times that average, appears at threshing. But policing the tenants' harvest closely has both economic and political costs that discourage both landlord and overseer from going too far, or, alternatively, encourages owners to consider evicting tenants and shifting to hired labour. Being caught at concealing the harvest could become legal cause for eviction of a tenant, which discourages tenants from going too far, or, alternatively, encourages them to use stratagems that are hard to detect.

Policing the harvest is very difficult if the reaping is done in wet weather, when it is imperative to thresh immediately lest the grain sprout or rot. All the harvest procedures from reaping to bundling, gathering, threshing, winnowing to measuring must be done in wet weather within a couple of days. Therefore a large workforce divided into many small teams is involved. There may be several teams on each of several farms, threshing and measuring at once. Neither the farmer, the overseer, nor for that matter the anthropologist can keep tally and track of the rice under such conditions.

Landowners try to discourage tenants planting at a time, or with a variety, that will bring out the reaping in wet weather. They want the reaping to take place in dry weather. Then the reaped rice can be left to sun dry on the stubble, in sheaves, and in stacks, until gathered into the *mandala* great stack to await machine threshing under scrutiny by the overseer of the whole of each farmer's crop, and the crops of all his tenants on that estate.[1] Provided that pre-threshing can be prevented by his overseers, the landowner believes more rice will appear at machine threshing for division. Moreover, that rice is already sun dried, ready for storage or sale. From the tenant's point of view this merely shifts his stratagems from the threshing back to the procedures between reaping and threshing.

The lowest-level overseers must live in the village if they are to be about at night to detect removal of sheaves from the fields and secret threshing. They are generally trusted tenants of the estate who receive some pay, cheap credit and other considerations from the estate for their duties. But they are tenants themselves with their own harvest to hide. As they are kinsmen, neighbours, *kumpare*, etc. of the other tenants, most want to avoid dangerous confrontations and maintain good relations with the villagers. Therefore threshing checkers and first-level overseers are generally content to not see, hear, or report anything provided it is not done too blatantly.

The *enkargado* managing overseer is not in such a difficult class or social position as the lower overseers, for he lives outside the village so that he is insulated against social ostracism and violence. He is usually a forceful man with a reputation for the capacity to effectively use violence. Moreover, he can develop his own intelligence sources – tenants currying favour over debts, informing on enemies, or receiving secret pay. A shrewd and fearless *enkargado* can catch out a tenant whose stratagems have been clumsy, for example:

> In January 1973 the enkargado of the Sevilla estate was in the village watching the threshing machine from his jeep, and making his presence obvious to tenants, preparatory to the *pagtutuos* 'reckoning negotiation' and drawing up the *tuid* statement of accounts, with each tenant for the 1972–3 crop. The Bo Captain said that the enkargado found straw from secret threshing that one tenant had been rash enough to put in his haystack. He browbeat the tenant into a confession, then had the Bo Captain called to witness it. The Captain estimates that he will not file charges, but will use this to frighten other tenants into revealing a higher *lugas* quantity of rice that 'fell out' before threshing by the estate's threshing machine. He will use the confession to be very strict with this tenant on recovery of debts.

A couple of days later, I was standing talking with a group of tenants; one said that 'someone' (possibly the first tenant caught, in return for leniency) has reported to the enkargado that another tenant present had shifted sheaves from the far end of his farm onto a kinsman's farm adjacent, on another estate, and in the next barrio. This puts that tenant, and his neighbour, the first level overseer, in difficulty. The enkargado joined us. First he talked generally about the state of the crop, land reform, politics. Then he turned to me. Does the International Rice Research Institute know what is the worst sickness of rice? No! Well its theft! The tenant reported for removing sheaves stooged for him, saying its the up and down sickness – imitating threshing movements. His neighbour the first-level overseer said nothing. The enkargado again used me to direct barbs at the others. Next year he will use me as overseer – a hint that he considers these two were in complicity, so the overseer had better report his neighbour or risk losing his job? He then complained of the tenant caught with tell-tale straw. What sort of fools do they take him for? When he inspected the crop before reaping that tenant said that his BE3 variety was performing badly, so he will revert to IR20. Now, when he is caught with the distinctive yellow straw of BE3 in his haystack, he claims to have threshed for seed! The enkargado does not need informers, they betray themselves by underestimating him. During the growing season they come borrowing rice for food. But as soon as the crop is ripe, they stop coming. Then they deny threshing secretly! Son of a bitch, he remembers these things! Now they reveal very small crops and claim they can't repay debts. This is a strange sickness of the rice – that it looks good before reaping, but is very poor at threshing. Son of a bitch he knows more about this sickness than does IRRI!

The tenant and enkargado then went to the latter's jeep, out of earshot. They had a long tense conversation. In the *tuid* statement this tenant revealed several cavans as *lugas* additional to what had come out of the threshing machine and was allowed to keep only 10 cavans.

Stratagems for Under-reporting the Crop

Under strict management the first-level overseer is supposed to tally the number of sheaves in each paddy as the harvest proceeds down the farm, and to produce a total sheaf count for the farm. He may then have a number of sheaves test-threshed by hand under supervision. This provides the tenant with his legitimate pre-threshed food and seed allowance, but it is accounted as *lugas* ('fall-out') that must be added to the machine threshed grain, to take the *kabuoan ani* ('harvest total') for the farm. The total appearing from the machine plus *lugas* should approximate the number of sheaves times the average yield per sheaf. But despite the overseers' inspection and tallies, and the head overseers' pressure to reveal pre-threshing during the agonistic *pagtutuos* 'reckoning negotiation' between *enkargado* and tenant to make up the *tuid* 'statement of accounts', a daring tenant can divert several sacks of grain as a 'sideline', by manipulating the sheaf tally and yield per sheaf.

(1) Reducing the sheaf tally: In all the operations below the farmer must rely on the discreet collusion of the harvest gang, if he has the post-reaping tasks all done by hired labour. The possibility of making a large sideline income from doing those tasks himself without having to trust the harvest gang affects whether some farmers hire labour on *atorga* to do all tasks, or on *laglagan* merely to reap and leave the rest of the tasks to the farmer.

The basic strategy is to make the sheaves hard to tally. One way is to make sure that in bundling sheaves they are not laid in rows and columns. The overseer may respond by asking how many sheaf ties were issued, broken, and left over, and therefore how many sheaves there are. The tenant (or harvest gang leader acting on his instruction) alters the figures so that fewer sheaves appear to exist. Should an overseer be so meticulous as to go out to the hot paddies and tally the sheaves in each, the tenant or harvest gang places newly bundled sheaves in the already counted paddies. Similarly, if the overseer waits to tally until the sheaves have been gathered into *sipok* and *talumpok* stooks on the bunds, the farmer removes what he can beforehand, then, although the number of stooks aligned on the bunds is easily counted, and each has a standard pattern and fixed number of sheaves, he can insert extra sheaves in the 'armpits' of the stooks, for removal later. The tactic detected in the instance above – placing one's sheaves on an adjacent farm – of another estate or owner, or one already counted of the same owner – is a variation.

In all these cases the farmer then removes sheaves down to the revealed number to thresh secretly. To avoid the tell-tale noise of *hampas* threshing, he may revert to the quieter old system of *giik* threshing by foot. In either case there is tell-tale straw to dispose of. In both the 1971–72 and 1972–73 harvests I noticed lots of straw floating in the river and at night the sound of hampas threshing in the yards of farmers whose own threshing had taken place weeks before. After the tungro-disease stunted rice plants in the 1971–72 harvest, hay was very scarce. Buffalo-owners were reluctant to waste it – a dangerous temptation. In the case above it was his effort to conserve scarce straw for buffalo fodder after the poor harvest (floods, then drought in 1972) that betrayed the farmer.

(2) Varying sheaf size: Even though a sheaf count has been made, there are various methods to remove part of the grain before the sheaves reach the threshing machine, hence the test-threshing under supervision, designed to establish average sheaf yield.

However, it is the tenant who makes the sheaf ties, *panali ng bigkis*, split from the outer layer of green bamboo. By making these in two lengths, then presenting the smaller sheaves for test-threshing, the tenant prepares to remove some grain from the big sheaves left in the field.

(3) Removing grain in hauling and stacking: In the various procedures for gathering in the harvest some grain inevitably shatters from the sheaves. Good husbandry dictates placing mats, etc. to catch it at places where the sheaves are likely to be handled roughly. The *tuid* settlement defines this as *lugas*, grain fallen out before threshing and requires that it be reported and added to the machine-threshed grain. A daring tenant places his mats, then at every handling of the sheaves dumps them heavily, grain end first, to maximise the fall-out. Given suitable varieties that shatter (grain detaching from the panicle) easily, he can make up to 20 cavans on a modal 2½ hectare farm during gathering-in.

The key sites to place mats where rough handling can spill grain are: in the buffalo cart, beside the intended site for *sipok* stooks, in the cart again, and beside the site for building the *mandala*. Before building the mandala the tenant makes a *patio* cleared floor surfaced with a slurry of buffalo dung to seal cracks in the ground, then tosses loose straw on this to keep the sheaves above any damp ground. By dumping the sheaves heavily in making the mandala, and treading their grain ends, he can dislodge more grain to fall to the bottom of the stack as sheaves are removed to feed the threshing machine. After the overseers depart, the tenant's wife may recover up to six cavans from the straw there. Grain got this way leaves no tell-tale straw. The battle of wits becomes a battle of wills at *pagtutuos* settling, when the tenant is under every pressure the overseer can muster to admit a high *lugas*.

(4) Distracting the overseer: During wet season threshing by *hampas*, and dry season machine threshing the tenant usually stays away from the threshing site. Takahashi [1969: 121, 122] noted this, and attributed it in Baliuag to a desire to make jobs for others, and to show trust in those threshing. In San Miguel these considerations operate, but are more often altruistic glosses put on a manoeuvre whose object is to free the male tenant to entertain and ingratiate himself with the overseer, so as to distract him from a careful tally, while the tenant's wife (or his mother or eldest daughter) polices the threshers and rethreshing gleaners and turns away poor women begging. It is culturally inappropriate for a man to be *kuripot* (stingy) or to be so *mahigpit* (strict) as to deny the threshers and gleaners their customary latitude. But a woman is admired for doing just what a man may not in these matters. Where he should be open-handed she is expected to be a careful guardian of the household stocks of rice and money. A woman can more directly tip out the grain of threshers and gleaners who try to exceed their share by hiding grain or colluding, whereas the man, apart from generosity, might invite violence by hinting at impropriety.

At *hampas* threshing, particularly in the wet season when there are several teams working separately, and therefore as many threshing sites (each swarming with *nanbabarog* ('rethreshing gleaner') who go over the exhausted straw), the threshers may collude with gleaners to throw them straw that has not been thoroughly threshed. The gleaners, under the guise of helping to remove leaves and foreign matter from the threshed rice, or of assisting in winnowing, manage to divert grain to *bilao* (winnowing) trays hidden under the straw.

At dry season *tilyadora* (machine threshing) the crew of the machine have a number of stratagems to divert rice during the running of the machine – they claim the first half sack to emerge from the machine after it begins on a farmer's stack, and after any stop caused by blockages. Those at the feeding chute manage to spill plenty of grain by handling the sheaves roughly; those at the delivery chute manage to spill grain and claim this later as *saping banig* (under the mat), not reported in the tally to the owner, along with any fraction of a sack at the end of the machine run.

During two years in the field I saw only one farm where no member of the farm household was present to watch the threshing, and this was a special case: the farmer was away working in another town; his wife running a store in another part of the village; his eldest daughter was supposed to watch threshing, but had been married against her father's resistance to his enemy's son only two weeks; moreover, the farmer was the then barrio captain, and leader of the dominant family in the village – and local elections were only a few weeks off, so that it was politically advantageous to be generously 'trusting' to the village poor.

At other wet season threshing sites in 1971, rethreshing gleaners were excluded from sites on the major estate after a tenant's wife remonstrated with gleaning women colluding with threshers. She forced the hand of the overseer who then barred all gleaners. In the 1971–72 dry season threshing, and again the following year, farmers' female delegates watched the machine crews closely, tipped out several half sacks of illegal grain, protested the excessive spills, and resisted generous *saping banig* distribution of the last, incomplete, sack. They protested that the farmer (these were the tungro and flood crop-failure years) was poor, debt-ridden, and had many children – justifications for turning away the landless (but stranger) threshing crew's appeals for generosity. The male farmer could not behave so. It would be culturally inappropriate. But more importantly, challenging the threshers' honesty could lead to violence on the spot, or a breach in the discreet relations that the male tenant builds up with the harvest team he favours with the right to work his farm and on whose collusion he depends for sideline stratagems against the landlord. Finally, the tenant's wife or other female delegate can turn away or give short measure to the village poor women, who stand about with their *bayong* baskets in the hope of being given a *salop* (three-litre) measure of rice out of *awa* (charity).

Meantime the tenant plies the overseer with drink and food, while ostensibly sitting in the shade making *panutos* (sack ties) of green bamboo. By getting the overseer in a convivial mood, he can create a situation where the count is loose, his wife can selectively reward those threshers, gleaners, winnowers, and village poor from the *saping banig* of each threshing team and keep a substantial amount of rice from it for herself.

(5) Colluding with the overseer: After all possible devices to conceal the true harvest from the overseer are exhausted, it is still possible to make a *kikbak* (arrangement) with him as *ka-isplit* ('co-splitters') to under-declare to the head overseer or owner what has been detected by the minor overseer. In the wet season harvest when there is no machine tally to contend with it is easier for either tenant or overseer to propose to the other a *kikbak*. The convivial atmosphere that the tenant sets up while distracting the overseer helps such a proposal to be delicately raised.

From the tenant's point of view the immediate gain varies according to his tenure arrangement. For instance, on 50/50 shares the tenant stands to gain four sacks (from the lands share), for every ten sacks understated if the overseer takes a *kikbak* of one sack. The other five sacks are already legitimately the tenant's. On 60/40 shares the tenant gains three from the ten; on 70/30 only two; on 75/25 only one-and-a-half, and on leasehold, nothing, provided that the harvest exceeds his fixed rent plus debts to the estate. However, if the tenant has large debts to the estate the calculation of his immediate advantage changes, for this is rice that cannot be seized for debt in the *tuid* settlement.

Overall, land reform laws that set the lease rent or purchase price of the farm in relation to average (revealed) harvest, and the effect of the HYV plus fertiliser and irrigation improvements combining to raise yields, give tenants of all kinds a long-term interest in keeping low the revealed harvest.

(6) Under-declaring the harvest to institutional lenders: Under tenancy the landowner recovers the land's share or rent plus principal and interest on loans at the threshing site. Given the built-in system of overseers he is in a position to know whether the harvest was within the normal range for each farm, or whether it was low because of weather or pest damage, etc. By law the tenant must be left no less than 15 per cent of the crop immune from seizure by the landlord for debt. In practice, this means that (if the particular landowner observes that law) the balance of debt plus a new round of interest accumulates against future harvests so that a tenant never has a good year in terms of his legally retained rice. Whatever his debts to the estate itself, it is frequently the case that the head overseer, who holds delegated authority to make and recover loans for the estate, may deny a tenant estate credit, but issue him a personal loan, that the overseer recovers on his own behalf during settlement. These loans are secured by the crop, and the collection procedure tied to threshing supervision and rent collection is difficult to evade.

Various government credit schemes – the FACoMa, ACA, ACCFA, and later government-sponsored rural banks and the Masagana 99 system, have difficulty in collecting loans. There are reasons internal to the organisations themselves: notably that many 'loans' are made to non-persons – fictitious borrowers who are in fact the officials themselves, or their friends and relatives. Other loans are made to non-farmers, with or without the collusion of the officials. After the 1972 floods certain officials in a northern Bulacan town manipulated their control of the distribution of flood relief, emergency agricultural loans, and crop-disaster write-off provisions, to make a tidy profit. They offered government emergency relief to the deeply indebted tenants of certain landlords, only on condition that they would sign for receipt of these plus disaster recovery loans from ACA. The officials deducted from the ACA loan the debt these tenants had to the estate, plus ten per cent for themselves, and paid the tenants only the balance. Thus the landowners recovered debts from a semi-rebel area, the officials took a profit, but the institution was left with irrecoverable bad debts laid to the account of farmers who had not received the money.

Other problems centre on the difficulty of inspecting the crop of a large number of borrowers to verify whether crop failure has indeed occurred to the level where write-off is proper, and the transaction cost and difficulty of collecting from many scattered small borrowers. But it is at least as important that farmers are happy to see institutional loans in the light of a government dole – a racket in which they might be lucky enough to profit from funds disbursed for political ends, as do the officials. Moreover, government credit is cheap, and comes to farmers who are already buried in high interest loans to landowners, stores, and village moneylenders. It is hardly surprising that they try to pay off high interest loans from pressing creditors first, and try any means to persuade officials to write off political loans or defer repayment. Any system like that adopted by ACA after the floods of 1972 and that depends on elective village officials to verify harvest failure is open to abuse. Any that depends on certification by fellow farmers who have the same interest in getting write-off, is foredoomed. It is curious that institutional lenders do not place their own checkers in the village or collaborate with landowners' overseers who are already there.

In short, farmers individually understate their harvest and collude as farmers and fellow villagers to claim harvest failure, so as to avoid the claims of institutional lenders and state irrigation systems.

(7) Under-declaring within the village: At crop division the village poor and village moneylenders try to exert claims on the rice that the landowner has let the tenant retain. The manipulation of what amount of rice the household lets it appear it has retained is the duty more of the farm wife than the tenant himself, although they work as a team. The sacks of rice exposed at the threshing site after the landlord's truck has hauled away rent and debt recovery are the public figure. Fellow villagers have a shrewd estimate of the sideline amount that has been already concealed. But the tenant, with a long face, remarks that the visible sacks are not really his – so many sacks were left for seed, so many are owed to creditors, and so on. Any sacks that are noticed in the house are attributed to a son's harvest pay on others' farms, or promised as return for seed swopped with another farmer.

The conventional stratagems are too many to detail. Among them are concealing the retained rice outside the house by lodging it with a village moneylender on deposit, while giving out that it was taken there to repay previous debts. Another is to sell it for cash to a village storekeeper who doubles as rice buyer in season, again explaining the delivery as repayment of debt. Rice kept in the house is usually concealed from prying eyes by storing sacks in the curtained-off *silid* (alcove) where the family's private possessions are kept, or spilling it from easily counted sacks into a *matong* (large woven bamboo store basket) whose variable sizes make it hard to estimate their volume, while a lid conceals the level of contents.

Village women who have given *purga* (purge gifts), and the village poor women begging, are the wife's responsibility. She complains that what appears to be the farm household's rice is in large part claimed already for pay to others, for debt, and food for her numerous children. Nevertheless she gives out some rice to related poor women, and those who have helped her prepare meals for farm labourers; she tries to reserve the gleaning opportunities for those who have such claim on the household by discouraging outsiders.

There are no witchcraft accusations levelled at a household that is noticeably ungenerous at sharing its harvest fortunes with those worse off. Other devices serve – the household is gossiped about, as having *masamang ugali* ('bad manners'); its members do not acquire a following of poorer relations and neighbours that could enhance their faction leadership chances; they find themselves uninvited to gatherings, and co-operative labour is difficult to find. Men want to give rice generously to others to win their support and a reputation that will serve them in the politics of exchange, but their wives and women folk want to retain as much rice as possible to turn it to lending and trading capital for buy-and-sell operations. A household in which husband or wife is incapable of skillfully playing these sex roles slips in the village, for each needs the other.

Stratagems of Resistance or Strategies of Survival?

The stratagems above advance the interest of the individual tenant-debtor at the expense of the landowner-creditor, but tactics to keep rice from class superiors are only part of a wider set whose object is to keep it for the household by evading or fending off claims by all other households. Peasants pursue diverse tactics to make ends meet and hopefully to accumulate enough to at least see their children established with a decent means of living. Whenever a tenant neglects the care of the crop to pursue off-farm work, sends his children to school rather than to weed the paddy, invests a fertiliser loan in pigs, a sewing machine or passenger tricycle, then family survival is advanced at the expense of the landowner or creditor. However, the pursuit of household interest, even at the expense of the landowner, and even when the action might on detection incur sanctions, does not seem sufficient to constitute 'resistance'. These are everyday forms of existence for peasants. Unless 'resistance' is spread to encompass all of everyday life, we must take account of the intent of the actor and of the moral and political evaluation of his class-mates.

Individual stratagems that allow tenants to survive by cheating on the overt terms of the tenancy relation may work to demobilise collective action to resist or change those terms. That the stratagems are illegal robs the tenants of that sense of outrage cherished by the just man unjustly treated, against the terms of tenancy and the landlords. It invites mutual distrust among tenants themselves for each must beware lest his neighbour secretly report his cheating in the hope of seeing him evicted and gaining the farm.

Landowners have been able to turn the prevalence of cheating to their advantage. The head overseer of a large estate outlined a battery of tactics that partly depend upon the cheating that is normal in a share tenancy relation. He acquired information and divided the tenants by assigning a larger farm, low interest loans, estate jobs, and other privileges to a tenant prepared to report on his neighbours. Where an efficient tenant was caught cheating he might be spared eviction in return for revealing the latest stratagems for concealing the harvest or actually denouncing accomplices and neighbours. He set traps for inefficient tenants in order to get rid of them legally. He tried to neutralise the threat of collective resistance by offering the larger farm of an evicted tenant to a villager who had demonstrated the will and capacity to organise tenants to petition for application of the 1963 land reform law in 1967. The landowners' association of the town delayed until 1981 valuation of their lands for purchase by the tenants or for leasehold under the 1972 land reform decree, by protesting that revealed harvests in the base years 1970 to 1972 were improperly low in the municipality because of massive cheating. Their object was to capture the windfall gains from multiple cropping and higher yields brought about after 1974 by massive World Bank investment to upgrade the irrigation system, by improved varieties, and by cheap institutional credit that allowed farmers to use more fertiliser.

What makes tenants' stratagems into 'resistance' is the conscious intent of some to cheat the system on the ground that a particular landlord or the tenancy system is unjust, plus concurrence by most of their fellows that it is right to evade unjust claims. All the tactics depend on the complicity of members of all classes in a village in a conspiracy that, despite the landlords' counter measures, is remarkably successful in concealing true harvests. This extended to a farmer who had got the courts, after several years' delay, to fix his rents in accordance with the 1963 law, so that he had little reason to conceal his harvest, but some desire to boast about the success of the farming methods of his son. He reduced his stated harvest in order to not cast doubt on that of neighbours. In arriving at a revealed harvest figure farmers take into account the obvious state of the crop, the overall level of harvest in the area, their own past harvests and so on, so as neither to look inefficient in comparison with neighbours nor have to sacrifice more than they must.

The gang of landless labourers and the winnowing-machine operator who handle the grain and are paid a share of their true tally, collude with the discretion of Swiss bankers in the figure announced by the farmer. They were rewarded in the early 1970s with monopoly rights to harvest that farm. Tenants who were known or suspected of reporting to the landowner were distrusted, excluded from secret meetings held to discuss the land reform law of 1971 and decree of 1972. Conversations stopped or changed when they approached. They were dismissed as *bata* ('hangers-on') of the landlord, vilified as *sipsip-buto* ('cocksuckers') and found it difficult to arrange exchange labour for final harrowing.

This degree of moral consensus among tenants of the two large estates that made up the bulk of the village area was absent among tenants of smaller landowners in the remaining portion. Tenants of large absentee landlords with whom they had no personal contact treated the relationship as an amoral conflict. Stratagems to advance their household interest at the owner's expense were restrained by little more than their evaluation of the risk of detection if they went too far. Tenants who had direct personal dealings with small town-resident owners regarded the relationship as something between a partnership and a lopsided friendship, governed by moral consideration in addition to circumspection.

NOTE

1. The tractor driven McCormick-Deering pattern threshing machine, used on large estates from about 1918, met its political demise about 1978. Once tenants gained confidence in the security of tenure under the 1972 land reform, they refused to use the landlord's machine. It was replaced first by hand threshing on the pattern of the wet-weather harvest. From 1979–80 farmers custom-hired new mini-threshers to break the harvest labour bottleneck and to crush labourers' resistance to a cut in harvest pay.

REFERENCES

Fegan, Brian, 1972, 'Between the Lord and the Law: Tenants' Dilemmas', *Philippine Sociological Review*, Vol. 20, Nos. 1–2, pp. 113–27.

Fegan, Brian, 1978, 'Establishment Fund and Čanging Class Structures in Central Luzon', *Canberra Anthropology*, Vol. 1, No. 3, pp. 24–43.

Fegan, Brian, 1979, 'Folk-capitalism: Economic Strategies of Peasants in a Philippines Wet-Rice Village'. Ph.D. dissertation, Yale University.

Fegan, Brian, 1981, 'Rent-capitalism in the Philippines', Research and Working Papers, Series No. 25, Third World Studies Center, University of the Philippines.

Fegan, Brian, 1982, 'The Social History of a Philippine Barrio', in Alfred W. McCoy and E. de Jusus, (eds.), *Philippine Social History*, Quezon City: Ateneo de Manila University Press.

Hobsbawm, Eric, 1965, *Primitive Rebels*, New York: W.W. Norton, 1965.

Hobsbawm, Eric, 1969, *Bandits*, London: Weidenfeld & Nicholson, 1969.

Ileto, Reynaldo C., 1979, *Pasyon and Revolution: Popular Movements in the Philippines, 1840–1940*, Quezon City: Ateneo de Manila University Press.

Kerkvliet, Benedict, 1977, *The Huk Rebellion*, Berkeley: University of California Press.

Mauss, Marcel, 1954, *The Gift*, New York: The Free Press.
Murray, Francis J., 1972, 'Land Reform in the Philippines: An Overview', *Philippine Socio-logical Review*, Vol. 20, Nos. 1–2, pp. 151–6.
Sahlins, Marshall, 1974, *Stone Age Economics*, London: Tavistock Publications.
Takahashi, Akira, 1969, *Land and Peasants in Central Luzon*, Tokyo: Institute of Developing Economies.

Everyday Resistance to Injustice in a Philippine Village

Benedict J. Tria Kerkvliet*

INTRODUCTION

One day in 1978 after my wife and I had settled into San Ricardo, a village in Luzon's central plain, I watched Tom, a ten-year-old boy lugging a bucket of water toward a ramshackled outdoor toilet.[1] Behind him toddled his younger brother, whining at Tom to wait. 'Just a minute! Stay there!', Tom shouted over his shoulder. 'I'm going to the bank to make a deposit.' That, I thought to myself, is a weird expression. Noticing a slight grin on the face of Nana Mina, Tom's grandmother, I wondered what I was missing.

Tom shyly told me later he picked up the expression from his father, Pepe Cruz. A man about my age (mid-30s), Pepe is a self-confident, likeable fellow. When I asked him about the metaphor, he laughed and explained that others use it, particularly men with whom he sometimes works as a construction worker. As Pepe responded to my probing about the expression's origins, he revealed it was – or at least could be – more than a casual remark. He would like to save money for depositing in a bank but whatever cash he manages to get, he and his wife and four children readily spend in order to eat and keep a roof over their heads. He works irregularly, his wages are small, and the prices he gets for whatever *palay* (unhusked rice) he sells are low. 'So, what do I have to deposit? Just my shit.'

Here then is a wisecrack that suggests envy, self-pity, and disgust. The 'disgust' part is particularly pertinent here. Obliquely he was saying that he deserves better wages and that prices he gets for the grain he sells are unfairly low. Uttering it, in short, is potentially and on occasion, actually *is* an act of resistance, however feeble, to what he perceives as unjust but too difficult to rectify.

While studying in a Philippine village for eleven months in 1978–79, I tried to be aware of various ways people might indicate discontent with their conditions.[2] Because it was only one of several concerns I had while trying to understand how villagers deal with and perceive socio-economic and political

*Department of Political Science, University of Hawaii, Honolulu, Hawaii 96822. A previous version of this article was prepared for a workshop on 'Everyday Forms of Peasant Resistance in Southeast Asia' funded by the Social Science Research Council (New York City) and hosted by the Institute of Social Studies, The Hague, in December 1982. The discussions during that gathering have helped me to revise. I am also grateful to Michael Adas, Bruce Cruikshank, Manfred Henningsen, Norman Owen, Werasit Sittitrai, Jayne Werner, and Willem Wolters for their supportive but critical comments on the earlier version.

changes during the last several decades, I surely missed much on this subject. Inspired by Michael Adas's [1982] and James Scott's [n.d.] fine analyses of resistance in South-east Asia that falls short of the rare but more often studied organised and headline attracting unrest and revolt, I have tried to discover the bases upon which people justify to themselves and possibly to others the hostile, angry, or indignant reactions they have to what other people or institutions do to them.

DEFINITION

Everyday resistance refers to what people do short of organised confrontation that reveals disgust, anger, indignation, or opposition to what they regard as unjust or unfair actions by others more wealthy or powerful than they. Stated positively, through such resistance people struggle to affirm what they regard as just or fair – or less unjust, less unfair – treatment and conditions. They are expressions of people who perceive injustice but for various reasons are unable or unwilling to push for improvements in an organised, direct manner. These reasons generally include the perception that they lack sufficient control or power or that the effort to gain more power in order to be more assertive would be too costly to themselves, their families, or other valued resources and conditions. They are, or at least consider themselves to be, limited to activities that indirectly, surreptitiously, or obliquely attempt to gain some of what they regard as rightfully theirs.

This definition only includes acts against or at the expense of individuals, groups, or institutions of or symbolic of better off or more powerful classes than those who are resisting. Excluded are protests against people in the same socio-economic strata – such as a tenant farmer, angry at a neighbour (also a tenant) who persistently diverts more than his share of water into his rice paddy or surreptitiously harvests some of the neighbour's grain. I am also excluding disgust and anger vented between a husband and wife, among siblings, and between children (for example, rebellious teenagers) and parents. Finally, I am not talking about what upper-class people do when they become upset by what they perceive as unfair actions of lower-class people.

By definition, everyday resistance is done by individuals and small groups with little leadership. Resistance that involves co-ordination among large numbers of people and a set of leaders is not 'everyday'.

What is resisted are often specific individuals or institutions such as a certain moneylender, landowner, government official, or governmental agency, but it can also be a general condition. To the extent the target is rather specific, those who resist imagine that their actions would not be condoned by the target.

My definition includes what Michael Adas [1982] has called 'avoidance protest' as well as other actions. If I understand Adas correctly, for something to count as avoidance protest, it must harm the target and both the one resisting and the target must be aware of this harm.[3] Adas also takes pains to distinguish between avoidance protest and acts that are 'defensive' or seek 'advantage' for the actor. I am arguing that there is a second category of everyday resistance about which the target is not necessarily aware. The target may eventually discover what the resister has done but that need not be the intention of the ones resisting.[4] Indeed, those resisting, often perceiving themselves to be extremely vulnerable, try to avoid leaving signs or evidence of what they are doing. An example could be harvesters pilfering produce from a landowner. They do not want the owner to discover their deed because that could mean expulsion from the field and even being forbidden to return the next season. They consider the portion that they are being paid is unjustly low but, being desperate for work, they accept. Later they try unobtrusively to get some of what they regard as fair. Everyday resistance may also be to one's advantage. The harvesters in the example improve, however minuscully, their household's food situation. Whether the resister benefits or is being defensive should not be the issue. What is central is that his or her action be an effort to resist perceived injustice.

The broad notion of everday resistance means that language usages that would not qualify as avoidance protest might be forms of everday resistance. Jokes, puns and other play on words, verbal characterisations, and even swearing and complaining safely in the confines of one's family and friends can reveal disgust and indignation with the way things are compared to how they should be even though the latter may only be dimly conceived. Drawing our attention to such speech acts is the literature on slaves and other oppressed people's resistance that falls short of organised and confrontational protest (see Levine [1977: 54, 240, 358]).

That literature also suggests four additional types of actions where we might look for daily resistance: various forms of deceit, footdragging, and what slaves called 'taking' [*Genovese*, 1976: 599–612]; cultural groups and institutions such as religious practices [*Genovese*, 1976: 212, 283, 659]; physical harm to property or persons, such as arson, sabotage, and ambush (see Elson [1979]; Genovese [1976: 613–17]); and forms of 'flight' such as leaving an oppressive landlord, running away, and walking off the job (see Price [1979: 3]; Genovese [1976: 648–57]; Adas [1981: 232–4]).

These five types of everyday resistance form a rough continuum from mild to strong in terms of likelihood the target is aware of what is being done, degree of harm to the target, and of danger or risk to the actor. Those acts at the mild end are more 'everyday' than those at the strong. Sabotaging harvesting machinery that has displaced workers, for instance, lies toward the 'stronger' end of the continuum. The machinery owner will likely discover what has happened, the material cost is probably substantial and he will probably try hard to catch and punish the saboteur. While not literally an 'everyday' act, it still probably occurs more frequently than overt resistance involving many people and shares with other everyday forms the characteristics of being non-confrontational and involving relatively little organisation.

These types do not necessarily form a continuum of degrees of consciousness from, say, simple to more complex explanations for one's situation. Machine breakers are not necessarily more aware than those who privately make up little ditties ridiculing the machine owners. The kind of everyday resistance that occurs corresponds more to what the oppressed think is possible than to what they understand about their situation.[5]

Although identifying resistance acts might be easy, often it is difficult to distinguish everyday types from convenience or an excuse for an actor's failing. If a man quits working for an employer, does it mean the man is fed up with abuses heaped upon him? Or does it mean he has found better employment, or that he is just tired of working at this place (maybe, for instance, because it requires him to travel great distances each day)? Even the man's own explanations are not necessarily adequate to distinguish resistance from something else.

To find out, the inquirer must explore possible meanings for the actions and understand their context. The more that can be reconstructed through documents, conversations, and observation, the more likely one can reasonably sort out what is what because he or she will be better able to make what Gilbert Ryle calls 'thick description' rather than 'thin description' [1971: 474–96]. The thin description captures the obvious; thick description adds the more obscure and hidden and consequently refines the meaning and significance of the observed – for example, conditions surrounding a worker's departure, her thoughts and intentions, his explanations and those of others, and so on.

Such inquiry even if extensive is inevitably constrained and the evidence often mixed; the researcher ultimately makes judgments and interpretations, which cannot be definitive. Regarding Pepe Natividad's euphemism, for example, I am not certain another participant observer would come to the interpretation that I have presented. Perhaps I would have seen less to the remark and Pepe's explication had I been ignorant of other aspects of his life – his conflicts with certain construction company owners and foremen, his scepticism of government promises to improve peasantry's livelihood, and his family's meagre means. He may not have revealed other possible layers of meanings had I not pried and, despite efforts to avoid leading questions, I might have steered Pepe in a direction he would not have taken were he talking with someone else. Even in another mood or another time, the conversation might have turned out much differently.

Still, I offer the utterance as an example of everyday resistance – at least for that time and place. Whether Pepe saying the expression today, four years later, would have the same thickness, I cannot say without looking and listening again. Already for his son Tom in 1978 it was just a way to say going to the toilet.

Most acts of resistance I have in mind while writing the following pages are not as difficult to perceive as was Cruz's remark. But frequently their bases are, and it is to this question I have attempted to offer tentative answers.

CONTENDING VALUES

In a stimulating search for universal conceptions of injustice, Barrington Moore, Jr., argues that within any society there are disagreements about how to solve three central problems – authority, division of labour, and allocation of resources.

> Several principles might very well be discernible in the workings of any one society, even a quite simple one ... In a larger and more complex society it would be natural to expect that different sectors of the population owed allegiance to different principles and that there were huge differences in the extent to which various people were consciously aware of these principles or could put them into words [1978: 11].

The same idea is central to W.F. Wertheim's argument that societies are composites of conflicting values, including two broad categories, dominant and counterpoint, the latter being potentially a basis for resistance and protest leading to social and political change [1965: Ch.2; 1974: 108–14, *passim*]. Wertheim goes on to argue that one of the social scientists' jobs is to look especially for those beliefs that do not readily meet the eye and that people themselves might not directly express possibly because of subjugation or they are not fully aware.

The idea of different, conflicting values, with some being more dominant than others, helps to describe aspects of San Ricardo society in Central Luzon and probably Philippine society in general. Limiting myself to the distribution question, I think a reasonable generalisation would be that Philippine society embraces a cluster of values encouraging individuals and their families to accumulate material goods and thereby enhance one's social standing. Such ideas are embedded in the meaning of *umunlad* (to progress) and *umasenso* (to rise, ascend – as in, to rise in status), which residents of San Ricardo and neighbouring areas generally say with approval or envy to depict others who are climbing the ladder of success. 'Success' is strongly associated with material comforts, college degrees, good jobs, and is a goal to which many aspire, although most believe that few can achieve it. Socioeconomic inequality is a given in these values.

Such acquisitive measures of one's worth probably correspond to aspects of early Tagalog society in which power and material comforts were distributed unequally [*William Scott*, 1982: 96–126]. They are also compatible with, partly derived from, and reinforced by the cash economy, private property, and other facets of modern capitalism. From radio and television advertisements to invocations from national government agencies hailing growth and development, San Ricardo residents, like most in the country, are deluged with messages that success and prosperity means family-size

Pepsi, Hitachi refrigerators, Crown Toyotas, and sprawling California-style houses in suburbia – roughly in ascending order.

But there are alternative, contending ideas, including relatively new ones regarding equality – if not in wealth (although this, too, has proponents) then at least in social and political treatment ('rich or poor, everyone should be treated alike') – as well as much older ones regarding obligations of communities to help poorest members and that people should share their success with others. These, too, are sometimes reinforced and espoused by religious and governmental authorities, but the most publicly vociferous advocates of such ideas are individuals and groups that the central government often regards as illegitimate or of questionable legitimacy – 'radicals', 'communists', and 'religious fanatics'.

Two contending values for which there is evidence from several parts of the Philippines are that people are entitled to be treated with dignity and entitled to livelihood. I shall refer to these as entitlement norms. Writing about the concept of justice in Filipino ethics, Leonardo Mercado argues that dignity is critical to Filipinos regardless of one's economic status [1978: 66, 82]. Other scholars also emphasise that the right to self-esteem (*amor proprio*) and humanity (*pagkatao*), whether among equals or unequals, is central to the society [*Lynch*, 1968: 15–18; *Guthrie and Azores*, 1968: 22–3]. Both are related to *hiya* (shame; sense of propriety) which Mary Hollnsteiner says regulates in lowland Philippine society 'the give and take of reciprocal and, in general, all social behaviour' [1968: 31]. 'He who is *walang hiya*' (shameless; lacking a sense of social propriety), writes Vitaliano Gorospe regarding Filipino morality, 'has no sensitivity to the privacy and delicate feelings of other' [1977: 282].

The right to livelihood is also endorsed in Tagalog and other Philippine cultures (see Guthrie [1970: 43]; Szanton [1972: 127–31]; Silliman [1982: 232, 242]).[6] As human beings, people are entitled to a means of making a living; and those who have more should share with those who have less (see, for example, Lynch [1968: 19]; Hollnsteiner [1968: 25]). Those who are better off are especially encumbered to assist those with inadequate means to live decently. This right to livelihood, therefore, places restraints on how resources should be distributed and how much people should accumulate for themselves.

These entitlement norms, however, are ambiguous. What exactly constitutes livelihood, dignity, and, bringing them together, livelihood with dignity? The better-off should help, but what constitutes help? There is considerable room for interpretation. In political terms, this means probing, testing, and struggle among those with alternative, often conflicting sets of values and interpretations about how values should be practiced. Here we can find everyday resistance by slaves, urban poor, peasants, death camp prisoners, and other oppressed peoples who, because of their situation must render unto Caesar what is Caesar's but also try to define *what is* Caesar's (see Genovese [1976: 658–60]). Frequently underlying their resistance are their conceptions of livelihood and dignity, rights to which not only poor Filipinos claim.[7]

BACKGROUND FOR EVERYDAY RESISTANCE

In order to appreciate the context in which everyday resistance occurs, I shall highlight six points. First, society in San Ricardo has become much more complex than it was one or two generations ago when most residents were share tenants growing rice and the remainder were mainly small landowners and petty traders. Now only 45 per cent of the village's 230 households (about 1,400 souls) have fields, mostly on a leasehold tenancy basis. Moreover, nearly half of these landholders hustle for additional sources of income in and beyond the village. Another big change is that about one-third of the village's households depend heavily on finding work as agricultural labourers; about half of these also manage to have household members who have some low-paying employment usually at construction sites outside of the village. The remaining roughly 20 per cent of the households include a few regularly employed construction workers' families, households that depend principally on petty trading, a handful of professionals, and a few large landowners whose fields are worked by others and who have other investments (real estate, businesses, etc.).[8] Economic diversity, competition for scarce work, and frequent moving in and out of the village has made such community customs as mutual aid and exchange labour difficult to sustain.

Second, paternalistic relationships that once characterised relations between large landowners (landlords) and share tenants are nearly gone. One reason is that they began to deteriorate rapidly in the 1920s–30s as landlords became more eager to increase production for expanding rice markets.[9] Another reason is that share tenancy is now the exception rather than the rule. Most tenant farmers in San Ricardo and vicinity are leasehold (*namu-muwisan*). Rather than giving the landowner a certain percentage of the harvest as share tenants did, leasehold tenants pay a fixed amount (in cash or *palay*). This means landlords can make no claims on tenants (other than the rent), but it also means that, unlike before, tenants can make no claims on them. It also means landlords contribute only land to production; before they paid all or part of such costs as transplanting. Consequently, virtually all the expenses and risks of rice farming now rest on the tenant.

Third, within the last decade, new hybrid varieties of rice have almost completely displaced previous seeds. The new varieties require enormous, by most growers' standards, amounts of cash (especially for chemical fertilisers and insecticides). No longer is it enough to have land in order to grow a decent rice crop; one must have capital. But capital is scarce, partly because prices for rice after harvest are low, so competition for it is intense and interest rates from moneylenders are high.

Fourth, poverty is widespread. About 30 per cent of San Ricardo's households live virtually hand-to-mouth. Most are landless with two or more members trying to find seasonal agricultural work as well as occasional wage labour on construction sites or in someone else's home. They also forage. Another 60 per cent are less poor; at least they usually have enough rice and vegetables to avoid hunger and frequently have cash to meet small necessities. For big expenditures or emergencies, they need to borrow. They are mainly landed households with members who also find other means of income; some are landless households with members who have regular wage earning jobs (usually outside of the village). Only about ten per cent of the households have ample food, well-constructed homes, and otherwise enjoy some comforts of life. A few here are very wealthy even by urban standards.

Fifth, San Ricardo, like many Central Luzon villages, was in the thick of unrest that grew in the 1930s as peasants protested against landlords who changed the terms of tenancy and against the government for supporting the landlords. This evolved into the Huk rebellion, which dominated politics in the region between the mid-1940s and mid-1950s [*Kerkvliet*, 1977].

Sixth, although no soldiers or police are in San Ricardo and its vicinity, people know that the central government can swiftly react to visible, organised signs of discontent. And, villages generally hold, the government is run by and for the benefit of well-to-do sectors of society.

The significance of these points is that even though the need for better living conditions is great, it is not clear to people where and how claims to livelihood with dignity can be made. Many previous customs helping to assure at least subsistence have disappeared with the demise of paternalistic relations with landowners and the increased complexity of society. More-over, because cash and capital have become necessities, sheer subsistence is often inadequate for one's livelihood. The Huk legacy remains an inspiration to many villagers, as a period when 'little people' organised against op-pression, but it was easier then to identify the oppressors – unscrupulous landlords, vicious soldiers, the police. Now it is often unclear who or what is to blame for impoverishment and degradation. Besides, during the rebellion many died and suffered tremendous hardship. The price for standing up was high and would undoubtedly be so again were villagers to attempt to organise today.

ENTITLEMENT NORMS

Asked what constitutes justice and injustice, San Ricardo residents are as likely to look perplexed or reply vaguely as they are to answer directly. But by analysing what people do and their explanations for their actions, one can begin to distill elements in their conceptions of justice. Two sometimes related ideas – that people are entitled to livelihood and to dignity – can be gleaned from what people say and do about others whom they regard as having more means or higher status.[10]

Language is one place to look. The better off people whom poorer people describe as nice, considerate, humane (*mabait, nagbibigay ng konsider-asyon, maykapwa tao*) are those who, for instance, give a little extra palay to harvesters, loan money and rice at low interest, and help poor neighbours repair their homes after a heavy storm. Other better off people are tight-wads, stingy, too strict, unconcerned, selfish, greedy (*madamot, kuripot, masungit, mahigpit, walang kusa, kamkamero, sigurista*). They measure the palay exactly so as not to pay harvesters any more than the agreed amount, refuse to make loans, charge high interest rates on loans, or ignore destitute neighbours. Such people may also be *mata pobre* – they look down on those less fortunate than themselves, treating them like dogs rather than like human beings.

People are not always one or the other. They may be seen negatively by some yet positively by others. And people sometimes act as though they want their cake and eat it, too – complaining, for instance, when someone tries to charge them a high interest rate but later, when they have money to lend, trying to charge someone else that same high interest rate.

Generally, it is to one's advantage to have a favourable reputation among several people with less means. Otherwise, in the words of one middle-aged tenant farmer, 'that stingy fellow [who has means] is likely to be picked on, stolen from, even hurt by the poor people'.

For instance, two Tinio families, large landowners who evicted numerous tenant families in the 1950s–60s in order to mechanise farming operations and whom many in San Ricardo regard as the epitomy of selfishness and insensitivity, no longer live in the village but do maintain large houses where family members stay while visiting their hacienda. But they will not remain in the area after dusk because, as some villagers said, 'they wouldn't dare', or as one Tinio member told me, 'it's too dangerous'. This man also said that unless the family hires guards (usually not from the area) during harvests, San Ricardo people 'rob us blind', sneaking into the vast fields at night to harvest. Confirming this to me, several villagers explained that they are not stealing; they are 'just taking' a little rice because 'we have none ourselves' and because the landowning family 'is so mean'.

Loans of money or rice with interest rates that are 'too high' are, as one elderly tenant said wryly, the kind that 'don't deserve to be paid back'. One local moneylender went broke because, in her words, 'ungrateful borrowers' never repaid several thousand pesos she had loaned. She received little sympathy from others who tended to say that she deserves her fate because the interest rate she charged was extremely high. Many villagers, including some other lenders, claim that because of this woman's experience several lenders lowered their interest rates, fearing what happened to her would happen to them.

Another example of what a reputation can mean for better off people involves subtle struggle between landholders and palay transplanters (usually landless) over the quality of *miryenda* (snacks). When a landholder arranges through a *kabisilya* (labour recruiter and foreman) for planters, miryenda is not part of the agreement. But it is customary for the landholder to provide it at mid-morning and mid-afternoon. What the landholder serves is her choice. If the miryenda is cheap, planters may grumble, especially if they believe that the landholder can afford to 'be a little generous' and 'show some consideration' to the planters who are paid very little and, as one said, are 'breaking *our* backs to plant *his* field but *I* have no field to plant so *he* will never be breaking *his* back for *me*'. Others curse: 'I hope your field becomes choked with weeds' or 'may the rats eat all your palay.' Such complaints, usually not made directly to the landholder but as an aside or under one's breath, might embarrass the landholder or make her sufficiently nervous to prepare a better miryenda in the afternoon than was served in the morning. In 1979 complaining planters in a couple fields went so far as to refuse to resume planting the fields of stingy landholders and marched to the fields of owners who were giving tasty miryenda.

There are, of course, limits. Transplanters who drag their feet when working for a landholder serving lousy miryendas might be replaced next time with others more desperate for work who will settle for a glass of water. And if no planters in the immediate vicinity are to a landholder's liking, others might be imported from distant villages. The same goes for harvesters and other landless workers. Landholders, though, who do ignore landless villagers can expect to hear about unflattering names that they are called or even to discover one morning that part of their field was harvested during the night.

Struggle involving entitlement norms is also reflected in other problems between transplanters and landholders. Landholders, sometimes overly anxious about getting their fields planted quickly or extremely wary of slackards, can become careless about how they speak to transplanters, calling them lazy, stupid, or worse (for example, devils, animals). Or they might harshly criticise some workmanship. Transplanters often respond to such rudeness by purposefully planting sloppily or slowing down. There are also instances of planters abruptly leaving the field and refusing to return until the landholder apologises for denigrating them. The same kind of thing can occur in other work settings such as distant construction sites where San Ricardo residents are sometimes hired. Several men have simply quit, even though they have no other work lined up, because they cannot tolerate being insulted. By footdragging and walking off the job, workers and transplanters are trying to protect their dignity and assert their right to be treated like human beings.

Entitlement norms are also expressed in controversies regarding land use. The two haciendas from which many tenants were evicted in the 1950s–60s have lately gone unplanted or only partially planted with sugar cane rather than *palay*.[11] The strong sentiment in San Ricardo is that 'it's not right' for land to sit idle while 'so many here are landless', reduced, as many say, 'to living like chickens' scratching about for kernels. 'We're not saying we should be given the land', explained a bitter landless man while he and others sat along the roadside talking about their situation. 'We just want to use it.' If they thought they could get away with taking over the land, they would. But, as one man surmised, 'if I started to plant some of Tinio's land, do you think I could last even a single week before he had me arrested and sent a bulldozer to destroy what I had done?' Twice in recent years fires have occurred in the sugar cane field. Arsonists did it, claim the Tinios, although they have not named names. Some residents indicate that arson is a possibility because there are people who are angry at the inconsiderate and greedy (*matakaw*) Tinios.[12]

By custom, pasturing one's goats and carabao, foraging for edible wild plants and shellfish, and gleaning after harvest are permissible in any unplanted field, no matter who owns it. Sometimes landowners try to interfere and say that people are 'trespassing' or are 'destroying the dikes'. Frequently people will leave but later, when the owner is not around, return to forage or pasture their animals. 'It is not right to keep me out', complained one lady who had defiantly returned to a field she had previously been told to leave. 'My family needs something to eat.' One landowner begrudgingly had to give up trying to keep others from pasturing their livestock in his unplanted field. His hired men were spending so much time enforcing his order to keep 'intruders' out of the fields that they had little time for actual work.

Entitlement is also expressed in justifications poor people have for taking from the better off. Chickens, goats, and pigs sometimes 'disappear'. So do vegetables, papayas, and bananas growing in people's yards. The victims are often the better off, although even the poorest must keep a wary eye on any pig or chickens they try to raise. Most residents agree that what is taken is probably consumed by hungry families in San Ricardo and nearby villages. This 'taking' can be a way for people both to assert their right to a livelihood and to blame better off people for their inpoverishment. Landlords and former tenants alike tell about how tenants used to take grain surreptitiously from fields prior to the actual harvest. Tenants justify this on grounds that their shares were too small or the landlord was too strict and lacked consideration. They also defend their deed by saying the landholder 'can afford' to lose a little grain.

A common activity that practitioners justify in entitlement terms is '*betsing*'. This refers to harvesters throwing into the discard pile stalks of *palay* that they purposefully thrash only partially, leaving many grains for a relative to glean.[13] Landholders have cited this practice to justify attempts to keep gleaners out of their fields. Knowing that if betsing were to become too extensive, all landholders would immediately burn the discard piles, harvesters exercise some restraint. Harvesters also generally want to have good relations with a landholder in order to be assured of harvest work next season. But harvesters who are desperate for food, as they frequently are after several weeks with no or little work while waiting for the *palay* fields to ripen, will justify betsing by claiming a right to more than what the landholder has agreed to pay them. Otherwise they will not meet their immediate needs. Some are not proud of doing betsing and will describe what they do as cheating (*daya*). They might even curse the stingy landholders for forcing them to be deceitful. But they are not stealing (*pagnanakaw*). 'It doesn't hurt the landholder', one middle-aged landless worker said. 'There is plenty of *palay* left for that fellow and his family even after he pays all his farming expenses. What my wife and I get by betsing he doesn't really miss or need; we, though, need it. We have absolutely nothing.'

Another expression of the entitlement norm are reasons people sometimes have for not paying certain debts, rents, and fees. An illustration concerns several *Masagana-99* borrowers. Started in the mid-1970s, Masagana-99 is a government programme to extend loans to peasants who cannot otherwise qualify for bank loans because they lack collateral. In the first year or two of the programme, about 30 landholders from San Ricardo had Masagana-99 loans. By 1979, however, only eight continued to qualify. The others no longer did because they had not fully repaid previous loans (the least amount owed was 500 pesos; several peasants owed two or three thousand pesos each). Their reasons were that due to poor crops (in some cases for two successive seasons) or extraordinary family expenses (usually large medical bills), they had considerably less income to meet family needs and to pay all claimants. Unable to supplement significantly from other work and unwilling or unable to reduce household expenditures and consumption, these families decided not to pay some of the claimants. Deciding which ones not to pay involves several considerations including personal relationship to those owed, geographical proximity of the creditors, likelihood of negative repercussions of not paying, positive benefits of paying, and the legitimacy of the claims.

Regarding unpaid Masagana-99 loans, two or three matters were especially compelling as people pondered what to do. Expecting that many households throughout the province would be unable to pay, villagers surmised – correctly – that the banking and governmental offices lacked adequate staffs to track down most delinquents. Possibly Masagana-99 itself would collapse, as so many governmental programmes have. Some borrowers also thought the government might or *should* give them consideration and not demand repayment. Especially important to many is their low regard for the Rural Bank through which they had received their loans. Besides having to wait weeks and make numerous trips to the bank before actually receiving the loan, they had to purchase the required fertiliser and other chemicals from a store owned by the bank's managing family, an illegal arrangement about which people felt powerless to do anything directly. Not repaying loans, so long as no repercussions came down on them, was a way to get back at the bank and the fertiliser store.

Significantly, people did not cut their family expenditures to bare bones subsistence in an attempt to meet all claims on their income. Some had no choice; the poorest of the landholders were already in that situation, having practically nothing beyond the most simple housing, food, and agricultural equipment. But several others lived better. Compared to the poorest landholders, they probably could have reduced expenses without going hungry had they wanted to pay their Masagana-99 loans. But they did not reduce drastically. They seem to be saying that they are entitled to what they have and maybe even a little more. They will not forego that in order to pay everything that was claimed of them.

The view that a family is entitled to more than subsistence and that claims should be somewhat flexible – take into consideration one's situation and needs with 'needs' being broader than bare minimum – is shared by others in the poor and not quite so poor levels of San Ricardo society. Such notions underlie Pepe Cruz's 'bank deposit' metaphor. They are also suggested when people complain about 'low prices we have to accept' for grain they sell, low wages they end up 'having to work for', and high prices they must pay for consumer goods, transportation, and other needs.

That livelihood is more than subsistence and hence is a claim others in addition to the poorest of poor can make is not simply an expression of envy for what others have or 'rising expectations' focused narrowly on material goods. There may be some of that but there is also a view of justice. It asserts that people have a right to live like human beings, not animals, and this means having enough resources in order to live with dignity rather than having to grovel and beg, to celebrate and appreciate life sometimes instead of having to scrounge daily for food because the rice bin is nearly empty and the money pot is depleted and no one in the household has an income, and to entertain reasonable hopes that the lives of one's children will be better.

CONCLUSION

The basis of everyday resistance highlighted in this article is that people are entitled to livelihood and dignity. These elements of justice have been strong in Tagalog culture. But norms need to be practised lest they become overwhelmed by others. In San Ricardo – and perhaps in many areas of the Philippines – there is a kind of friction due to entitlement norms rubbing abrasively against values that encourage individuals and families to scramble, with scarcely a glance sideways or downward to those they elbow and step on, to accumulate material goods and wealth and climb the ladder of success. Most villagers experience conflicting values within themselves and may attempt to act according to both. It would be incorrect to say that the better off hold the acquisitive values while only the poorer ones have entitlement norms. The everyday resistance discussed in this article, however, reflects poorer residents' efforts, based on entitlement norms, to qualify and shape their relations with those who are better off.

Practising entitlement ideas has been more difficult in recent years. A generation ago an important basis of landlord–tenant relations was that share tenants had a right to help from their landlords to meet subsistence needs. That system of land tenure is gone, however, and no longer do share tenants compose the bulk of society. Earlier, socio-economic divisions within the village and surrounding area were sharper, mainly between the numerous poor share tenants and the few rather prosperous landlords. Now distinctions are more gradual and complex. Hence, struggles involving entitlement norms frequently occur in unfamiliar contexts and among people whose socio-economic differences are less pronounced. It is not clear, for instance, to landless agricultural workers – now a significant percentage of the village population – how they can press their right to livelihood. Still, they try, for example, by secretly taking grain from those for whom they are harvesting, by attempting to determine some of the terms of their employment, and by contemplating how to use or even take over land whose owners are not farming it. Only in the last case is the target immensely better off than the landless people.

One pivotal question in studies of South-east Asian peasant politics is whether peasants struggle to retrieve what was or to reach for something new (see James Scott [1976]; Popkin [1979]). Many San Ricardo households seem to be attempting both, often simultaneously. Although many people share an image of a past wherein community was strong and everyone was assured of life's necessities, few hold much hope of restoring it. Yet entitlement norms do come from the past. But then so do rival ideas reinforcing self-enrichment and success. The meaning of entitlement, however, has not remained constant. Its content and how and where it should be practised have changed – are changing – with new influences. Villagers have been attempting not only to maintain a standard of subsistence that was appropriate for an earlier period but also to reach beyond it to some of what other sectors of society have long had and now take for granted but still deny to the majority, especially in the countryside. The idea that education, sturdy housing, sanitation, and regular income are necessities – something the dominant classes have long enjoyed – has worked its way into San Ricardo people's thinking and is beginning to be expressed in entitlement terms when villagers associate these with human dignity and decent livelihood.

This change in what villagers try to get may seem modest to readers who hold what are generally regarded as more progressive and radical ideas. Its modesty and the fact that people often settle for small concessions from more powerful and wealthy people or only do seemingly innocuous things against oppressors may lead some concerned readers to conclude that everyday resistance is of little or no political significance except to perpetuate an oppressive, unjust system.

I would suggest, however, that such a conclusion would be too narrow. First, everday resistance often brings important gains to the poor. While modest to us who enjoy a life of study and thinking, the miserably paid workers' acts of defiance often help them to assert their humanity and put rice on the table.[14] Second, the cumulative effects of everyday resistance can thwart the plans of those with more power and status. A small example from San Ricardo is that individuals' persistent day-by-day opposition to landowners who try to keep them from pasturing, gleaning, and foraging in fallow land has sustained these practices. Similarly, some owners' plans to expand their farms have been stymied over the years by residents who refuse to leave and encourage others to build additional houses. Allen Isaacman, *et al.*, [1980: 609–10] find that the effect of thousands of individual peasant families leaving certain localities, circumventing an imposed agricultural schedule, and otherwise resisting without directly challenging the state's cotton programme was to frustrate companies' plans and probably caused low yields. John Steinbeck [1942] vividly portrays the same phenomenon in his novel about people in a Norwegian town gradually wearing down the morale of occupying German soldiers by footdragging, sabotage, and other indirect resistance. Finally, everyday resistance may help to nurture ideas of justice that can be the basis for far-reaching visions and protest movements in another time under different conditions. Were the dominant order to falter seriously due to a political and economic crisis, entitlement norms might expand to encompass the images of liberation, fellowship, and equality that Reynaldo Ileto [1979] argues the *pasyon* – a religious ritual (still sometimes performed in San Ricardo) celebrating the life and resurrection of Jesus Christ – 'culturally prepared' Tagalog villagers to embrace as the Spanish regime crumbled in the nineteenth century. Such a crisis might permit those in San Ricardo who now only fantasise about taking over underused land to actually do it. In any case, the local conception of justice, of which entitlement norms are a part, is a starting point that, as Ralph Thaxton [1983] contends the Communist Party had to learn in the north China border region, others must take seriously in order to mobilise peasants to struggle for a less repressive and more just Philippines.

NOTES

1. Names of people are fictitious. San Ricardo is located in Nueva Ecija province, about 150 kilometres north of Manila.
2. For that research, I am grateful to the National Endowment for the Humanities and the University of Hawaii for financial assistance and to the Institute of Philippine Culture (at Ateneo de Manila University) and the College of Public Administration (at the University of the Philippines) for institutional support.
3. I am drawing upon Adas's excellent papers [1981 and 1982] and recent correspondence to me.
4. This is one reason why I prefer the term everyday *resistance* rather than *protest*. 'Pro' in 'pro-test' suggests 'forth', meaning 'out; into view, as from hiding or obscurity'. Resistance comes from 'resist', which includes the meaning 'to strive, fight, argue, or work against; to endeavor to counteract, defeat, or frustrate', all of which may be open or semi-open but may also be subtle and done without the one who is resisted being aware or at least not aware until considerable time has passed (*Webster's New Twentieth Century Dictionary*, second edition, 1971).
5. Post intimates the same point in his typology [1982].
6. Livelihood can be what James Scott [1976: 17] calls subsistence but, as I hope to suggest later, it might include a little bit more. 'Livelihood' is also the word found in some of the literature on Philippine values, although 'survival' and 'subsistence', too, are used.
7. Preserving and asserting one's dignity in the face of economic hardship and even extreme repression appears to be a basis for everyday resistance in many contexts. One reason Lawrence Levine says black people's songs can be a form of what I am calling everyday resistance is that through songs '... Negroes could be relatively candid in a society that rarely accorded them that privilege ... and, in the face of the sanctions of the white majority, could assert their own individuality, aspirations, and sense of being' [1977: 240]. Allen Isaacman, *et al.*, notes that peasants in colonial Mozambique engaged in several acts

of defiance (including certain songs as well as arson) '... to assert their own dignity and community strength and to validate their cultural identity' [*1980: 613–14*]. For survivors of death camps, Terrence Des Pres concludes, 'The need for dignity and the will to resist are closely related. They may in fact be identical: two ways of warding off capitulation, of saying No, of insisting upon the observance of a boundary between self and world' [*1976: 202*].

8. For more details, see Kerkvliet [1980].
9. For elaboration about deteriorating landlord–tenant relations in Central Luzon, see Larkin [1972: 204–39, 270–307]; Fegan [1979: 35–56]; and Kerkvliet [1977: Chs. 1, 2].
10. In this brief article, I cannot discuss other elements of justice and injustice on which everyday resistance is also sometimes based.
11. The two families have other businesses and investments that are more lucrative, engaging, and, as they say, 'less headache' than their haciendas. In addition, siblings in one family are quarrelling about whether to farm or sell the 200-hectare hacienda and how to divide either the land's harvests or the land itself.
12. Signs of discontent became serious enough in 1978–79 to prompt village officials to petition the Ministry of Agrarian Reform to subject the haciendas to land reform. Some in San Ricardo are hopeful this will succeed. More, however, doubt it will ever happen.
13. A likely origin of *betsing* is the word '*betsin*', a food seasoning. This would make sense here in that the harvesters are in effect 'seasoning' the discard pile for the benefit of those who glean (*nagbabarog*).
14. When assessing the significance of grain riots and other protests by poor people who were pacified with handouts and charity in early nineteenth-century France, R.C. Cobb writes, 'Historians, few of whom have ever experienced hunger, have no business blaming poor people for accepting, even gratefully, the produce of bourgeois charity ...' [1970: 320]. His point is well taken not only for that period and historians but for other times and places and other scholars.

REFERENCES

Adas, Michael, 1981, 'From Avoidance to Confrontation: Peasant Protest in Precolonial and Colonial Southeast Asia', *Comparative Studies in Society and History*, Vol. 23, No. 2.

Adas, Michael, 1982, 'From Footdragging to Flight: The Evasive History of Peasant Avoidance Protest in South and Southeast Asia', unpublished.

Cobb, R.C., 1970, *The Police and the People: French Popular Protest 1789–1820*, London: Oxford University Press.

Des Pres, Terrence, 1976, *The Survivor*, New York: Oxford University Press.

Elson, Robert E., 1979, 'Cane Burning in the Pasuruan Area: An Expression of Social Discontent', in F. van Anrooij, D. Kolff, J. van Laanen, G. Telkamp, (eds.), *Between People and Statistics*, The Hague: Nijhoff.

Fegan, Brian, 1979, 'Folk-Capitalism: Economic Strategies of Peasants in a Philippines Wet-Rice Village', Ph.D. dissertation, Yale University.

Genovese, Eugene D., 1976, *Roll, Jordan, Roll*, New York: Vintage.

Gorospe, Vitaliano R., 1977, 'Sources of Filipino Moral Consciousness', *Philippine Studies*, Vol. 25, Third Quarter.

Guthrie, George M., 1970, *The Psychology of Modernization in the Rural Philippines*, Quezon City: Ateneo de Manila University Press.

Guthrie, George M. and Fortunata M. Azores, 1968, 'Philippine Interpersonal Behavior Patterns', *IPC Papers No. 6*, Quezon City: Ateneo de Manila University Press.

Hollnsteiner, Mary R., 1968, 'Reciprocity in the Lowland Philippines', *IPC Papers No. 2*, Quezon City: Ateneo de Manila University Press.

Ileto, Reynaldo Clemeña, 1979, *Pasyon and Revolution: Popular Movements in the Philippines*, Quezon City: Ateneo de Manila University Press.

Isaacman, Allen, Michael Stephen, Yusuf Adam, Maria Joao Homen, Eugenio Macamo, and

Agustinho Pililao, 1980, ' "Cotton is the Mother of Poverty": Peasant Resistance to Forced Cotton Production in Mozambique, 1938–1961', *International Journal of African Historical Studies*, Vol. 13, No. 4.

Kerkvliet, Benedict J., 1977, *The Huk Rebellion*, Berkeley: University of California Press.

Kerkvliet, Benedict J., 1980, 'Classes and Class Relations in a Philippine Village', *Philippine Sociological Review*, Vol. 28.

Larkin, John A., 1972, *The Pampangans*, Berkeley: University of California Press.

Levine, Lawrence W., 1977, *Black Culture and Black Consciousness*, New York: Oxford University Press.

Lynch, Frank, 1968, 'Social Acceptance', *IPC Papers No.*, Quezon City: Ateneo de Manila University Press.

Mercado, Leonardo N., 1978, *Elements of Filipino Ethics*, Tacloban City: Research Center, Divine World University.

Moore, Barrington, Jr., 1978, *Injustice: The Social Bases of Obedience and Revolt*, White Plains, New York: M.E. Sharpe.

Popkin, Samuel L., 1979, *The Rational Peasant*, Berkeley: University of California Press.

Post, Ken, 1982, 'Everyday Forms of Peasant Resistance: Some Notes on Theoretical Issues and a Socialist Case', unpublished.

Price, Richard, 1979, 'Introduction', in Richard Price (ed.), *Maroon Societies: Rebel Slave Communities in the Americas*, Second edition, Baltimore: Johns Hopkins University Press.

Ryle, Gilbert, 1971, *Collected Papers*, Vol. 2, New York: Barnes and Noble.

Scott, James C., 1976, *The Moral Economy of the Peasant*, New Haven, CT: Yale University Press.

Scott, James C., n.d., 'Normal Exploitation, Normal Resistance', unpublished.

Scott, William Henry, 1982, *Cracks in the Parchment Curtain*, Quezon City: New Day.

Silliman, G. Sidney, 1982, 'The Folk Legal Culture of the Cebuano Filipino', *Philippine Quarterly of Culture and Society*, Vol. 10.

Steinbeck, John, 1942, *The Moon is Down*, New York: Penguin, 1982 edition.

Szanton, Maria Cristina Blanc, 1972, *A Right to Survive: Subsistence Marketing in a Lowland Philippine Town*, University Park: Pennsylvania State University Press.

Thaxton, Ralph, 1983, *China Turned Rightside Up: Revolutionary Legitimacy in the Peasant World*, New Haven, CT: Yale University Press.

Wertheim, W.F., 1965, *East–West Parallels*, Chicago: Quadrangle.

Wertheim, W.F., 1974, *Evolution and Revolution*, Harmondsworth: Penguin.

Plantation Politics and Protest on Sumatra's East Coast

Ann Laura Stoler*

Accounts describing plantation systems throughout the world, be they of the nineteenth-century American South, colonial Latin America, East Africa or contemporary South-east Asia, all allude – and seek some analytic resolution – to the fact that plantation economies rarely transform peasants and tribal populations into full-fledged proletarians but more often allow – and frequently *compel* – some degree of self-sufficiency on the part of their workers. In the American colonies, slaves were 'forced to grow some part of their own subsistence' [*Mintz and Price*, 1973], in Zanzibar they were permitted small food plots in exchange for a rent in labour [*Cooper*, 1980: 80], and in colonial Sumatra plantation coolies were assigned unused estate fields, at least in years of crisis, to cultivate consumption crops in their 'spare time'.

The ambiguous position of estate labouring-cum-food-producing populations on the estate peripheries of Latin America, Asia, and Africa seems to defy easy classification. Eric Wolf refers to their 'double lives, with one foot in the plantation way of life, while keeping the other foot in the peasant holding' [*Wolf*, 1959: 143]. Geertz similarly notes that 'the Javanese [sugar] cane worker remained a peasant at the same time that he became a coolie'; in other words, a 'part-time proletariat' with 'one foot in the rice terrace and the other in the mill' [*Geertz*, 1968: 57, 89]. Mintz thinks this cultural straddling was not a transitional mode at all, but a state of 'flux equilibrium', advantageous to management and labour alike [*Mintz*, 1959: 43]. More recent studies, such as Michael Taussig's on Colombian estates, calls these peasant-estate labourers 'liminal beings ... neither what they are, nor what they will become', whose cosmology reveals the ambiguous experience of dependence on 'two utterly distinct forms of life ... on two antithetical modes of production' [*Taussig*, 1980: 92, 103, 113].

'Liminality' may well describe this ambiguity but does not explain it. More to the point, we might question whether the *sustained* tension between peasant life and proletarian labour is really clarified by positing the ar-

*Department of Anthropology, University of Wisconsin, Madison, Wisconsin 53706, USA. The research and analysis for this study have been supported by a number of institutions: Social Science Research Council, Fulbright-Hays, NIMH (Training Fellowship #MH07395), and the French Ministry of External Relations. Earlier incarnations of this manuscript were presented in Februry 1983 to the Anthropology Seminar, University College, London and in March 1983 to a seminar on questions of transition at the Ecole des hautes études en sciences sociales. I would like to thank Rod Aya, Maurice Godelier, Lawrence Hirschfeld, Richard Lachmann, and Jim Scott for their careful readings and helpful criticisms.

ticulation of two modes of production? Indeed we may ask whether there are two modes of production at all. An answer would presumably require knowing what the two faces of this ambiguity actually represent.

For example, some students of plantation economy have attempted to explain this part-proletarian, part-peasant producer status as a cost-cutting device, arguing that peripheral capitalism tends to preserve those 'traditional' relations of production and exchange that serve its concerns.[1] According to this argument, capitalism does not destroy prior bases of subsistence but, on the contrary, 'coexists with them ... buttresses them, and even on occasions devilishly conjures them up' [*Foster-Carter*, 1978: 213].[2]

Others, however, interpret the part-time agricultural activities of plantation workers from a different perspective. Here the clandestine slave gardens on plantation peripheries, underground rural marketing networks stocked with produce from private slave plots, house and garden compounds intentionally established *outside* the plantation confines,[3] and seizure of squatter fields are seen as bids for economic independence grounded in popular *resistance* to capitalism itself [*Mintz*, 1974]; (see also Genovese [1976]; Price [1979]).[4] Mintz [1974: 132] in particular argues that this effort at agrarian self-sufficiency resulted in the 'reconstituted peasantries' of the Caribbean where their communities were 'a mode of response to the plantation system and its connotations, and ... a mode of resistance to its imposed styles of life'. The best known of these communities were the jungle-based *maroon* settlements of runaway slaves, who completely severed themselves from the mainstream of plantation work, and lived entirely off hunting, foraging, incidental agriculture and estate theft. In French Guiana the authorities labelled these villages the 'gangrene' of the industry, and in Colombia their economic independence was considered a political danger and a drain on the planters' labour supply [*Price*, 1979: 3, 105].

Are we to conclude from these discrepant interpretations that the subsistence efforts accompanying plantation work always represent *either* strategies of labour control required by capital *or* successful modes of popular defense? Posing the issue this way in itself suggests that the two effects are contradictory. The former implying that capital makes workers pay the cost of their own reproduction, the latter that labour sees to part of its own subsistence so as to assert its autonomy and resist – furtively or by force.

Yet the two interpretations are not in fact mutually exclusive. In what follows I argue that the very preservation, creation or reconstruction of a subsistence community arose from the contest for power and is explainable neither solely by its functional utility to capitalism nor by its defiance of it. As we shall see, in North Sumatra at least, the relationship between subsistence farming and wage labour, between proletarian and peasant priorities and identification, reveals a long-term oscillation in the relations of power and production at different moments in Sumatra's plantation history.

Tracing the changing strategies of labour control and confrontation should allow us to better understand how such communities became the focus of long-term and daily conflicts between the industry's effort to enforce, and labour's effort to resist, control over workers' lives. Historically we will be able to see how the companies succeeded in creating the semblance of village life on their peripheries, and why the workers repeatedly failed in transforming this into an independent agrarian base. How and where these workers would be allowed to live, work and reproduce was a pivotal issue of colonial capitalism and its post-independence transformation. The contemporary social, economic and political structures of North Sumatra owe much to how these issues of land and labour were settled, if not resolved.

This is apparent if we briefly examine some changes that accompanied the conversion of land and labour power into commodities and how the effects of these changes can be seen on North Sumatra's plantation periphery today. With this in mind, I turn to the opening of Deli, to the emergence of the estate industry and to its expansion, focusing on certain aspects of its growth that led to the development of the peripheral communities and the class positions of their inhabitants. In doing so I examine how the planters defined the *vraagstukken* ('issues') of property rights and popular resistance, and how the workers set limits to labour control.

JAVANESE ON THE PLANTATION PERIPHERY TODAY

Javanese villages now surrounding the large rubber, palm oil and tobacco plantations of North Sumatra vary significantly but share certain common characteristics.[5] These villages are located within Sumatra's 'plantation belt', an area reaching inland some 50 to 70 kilometres and stretching out 250 kilometres on a north–south axis, which today includes about 265 plantations totalling over 700,000 hectares in holdings, owned by a mix of state-controlled, joint-venture, and private foreign and national estate corporations.[6]

Unlike the plantation companies of Java whose expansion thrived on a workforce drawn from surrounding villages – in which a critical portion of that power was maintained and renewed – on Sumatra's East Coast, Chinese and later Javanese workers were imported by the hundreds of thousands, housed and fed in estate barracks, and bound by indenture. These 'contract coolies' were subject to a basic ordinance stipulating that in exchange for passage to Deli, a recruit was obliged to work a specified number of years. A strict penal code (*poenale sanctie*) enforced the harsh terms of these agreements.

Today, virtually all the inhabitants in villages on the plantation periphery are themselves former contract coolies, or descendants of them. Initially most of the former were enticed to Sumatra by the lure of a cash wage which they thought would allow them the savings to buy land on their return to Java. As we shall see below, simply managing to return to Java proved beyond the means of a large portion of the coolie population. For those who remained in Sumatra, the struggle has not been to amass the savings sufficient to buy land, but to find any means of disengaging from a purely wage-labouring status. Again as we shall see, this has centred on efforts to establish independent homesteads for small-scale agricultural production on land seized directly from the estates.

For their children, in contrast, employment as a permanent estate worker is a prized position, coveted by many but granted to only a small percentage of the young, healthy, often unmarried men. For them, villages are no longer agricultural centres at all, but estate-dependent residential wards housing them and their dependent parents. The remaining majority of the village members, male and female, old and young also work on the estates, but on a temporary basis, receiving a fraction of the wages, and none of the social benefits accorded their permanent counterparts. Yet these temporary estate workers, especially the youth, commonly disclaim any real ties to the plantations, and scorn – and systematically avoid – work on the small agricultural plots of their parents.

Contemporary Javanese villages on the plantation periphery are defined as much by their specific relations to the surrounding estates (from which they seized their holdings in the 1940s and 1950s) as by their ethnic link to Java. Social space and social time share this separation, with the temporal rhythms of work and leisure tuned to and dominated by the cadence of the industry. It is not that the Javanese have given up their *slametan* (ceremonial feasts), they have simply altered the criteria by which they decide to have them – according to estate pay-days rather than some divinational calendar. Current events are not dated by weeks but where they fall in relationship to the pay-day just passed or the one that is about to come.

None of this would be particularly surprising if it were not for the fact that such communities *appear* – and take themselves – to be so clearly separable from the estates. For example, the majority of their inhabitants refer to themselves as 'farmers' (*'tani'*), despite the fact that often more than half the households have no cultivation or ownership rights to rice land, and among those which do, only a handful actually support themselves from farming. In the village administrative unit in which I lived and which I will call here Simpang Lima, average landholdings between 1957 and 1978 fell from .40 to .13 hectares per capita. This was due primarily to the stream of estate workers and former plantation employees who moved into the community in the 1950s, but also to an increase within the community itself as mature children established their own homes and parental holdings were divided among them.

A retrenchment of tens of thousands of plantation workers in the late 1960s and early 1970s exacerbated population pressure in such villages all the more. Not only have fired workers been forced to find living space outside the estate compounds but since few of their children have found permanent estate jobs, they too have been denied access to estate housing and have been pushed out to the plantation periphery. Simpang Lima has not suffered as seriously as other squatter settlements. Many of these, formerly surrounded by dry- and wet-rice fields, have completely lost their agricultural base, and now exist only as rural residential complexes, housing a dense reserve of unskilled labour. Almost all of their inhabitants, children as well as adults, work as *buruh lepas* (temporary workers) under labour contractors for the estates.

What is most striking about the economic activities of Simpang Lima's inhabitants is the frequency and fluidity with which they change. The bulk of the population is continuously moving from one job to another as new opportunities open and others close down. Underemployed young men call this '*mocok-mocok*' (a term emphasising the varied nature of 'odd-jobbing') when referring to the wide range of activities one does in the absence of steady work. The most obvious difference between the work patterns of 20 years ago and today is that the majority of women and men are now not regularly employed. This does not mean that people work less. They just have to juggle a less reliable set of options which include local scavenging, temporary migration and theft – usually of estate produce.

Simpang Lima is thus not on any objective measure an agricultural community and certainly not a self-sustaining one. It is a rural ward, feeding the demands of North Sumatra's estate and regional labour market, and harbouring those workers between their forays into it. But they are maintained, not necessarily on the proceeds of agricultural production, but on wages earned by other household members in other sectors. What we are looking at then is a mode of consumption, not distinct from capitalism but part of it. Simpang Lima does support a specific *form* of production distinct from that of estate agriculture, but both the material and labour inputs on which it rests are either derived from, or maintained and reproduced by capitalist relations of production and exchange. Farming materials such as chemical fertilisers and insecticides are made by foreign and domestic industrial firms and purchased only with the help of wages earned on the estates. Agricultural labour inputs are minimal, often the part-time responsibility of older villages who in turn are largely supported by other wage-earning household members. The commoditisation of labour has meant that family labour is difficult to recruit even for the 'family' farm. Finally, Simpang Lima's *appearance* as an agricultural community is confirmed by the virtual absence of independent village-based relations of production concomitant with attenuated inter-household exchange.[7]

From the companies' perspective, these settlements seem to combine the best of all possible worlds. They certainly bear a close resemblance to what Deli's foreign planters envisioned as ideal labour communities some 50 years ago; namely, ones housing an abundant labour reserve in close proximity to the estates, but ostensibly outside the latters' ken or responsibility. In the form they now assume such villages serve the agribusiness labour market well, but this certainly has not always been the case. If anything they continue to exist in virtue of having always held a contested economic and political status in this changed multi-ethnic, multinational setting. What directions these communities have taken, how they have expanded and contracted, how they have been constrained from doing so, are, as we see turning back to the nineteenth century, basic questions informing the changing modes of exploitation and resistance in North Sumatra as a whole.

THE EARLY CONTOURS OF LAND RIGHTS AND LABOUR CONTROL

In 1880 East Sumatra's population of coastal Malays and the five Batak sub-groups was estimated at somewhere near 100,000. Fifty years later – with the inflow of Javanese, Chinese, Europeans and Indians working for the industry or in its service sectors – it had reached 1.5 million, with Javanese, mostly estate coolies, making up nearly 50 per cent of the native population [*Dootjes*, 1939: 50]. Of East Sumatra's 30,000 square kilometres of rich, alluvial lowland plains, more than 10,000 square kilometres – designated the 'plantation belt' – were concessioned, leased and brought under the control of the foreign plantation industry. Within 50 years of Deli's opening, the Sumatran industry's production of rubber, palm oil, tobacco, tea and sisal accounted for a third of the export earnings of the entire Dutch East Indies, providing many of the raw materials on which the expansion of late industrial capitalism in Europe and America was based.

Although Sumatra's East Coast was characterised (in colonial accounts) as a vastly underpopulated waste land, the politics of agrarian policy suggest otherwise. A 1918 map of the plantation belt drawn when company holdings were still being consolidated and enlarged, already reveals that little un-claimed land was left outside the estate borders. While in the tobacco area indigenous Malay residents had some access to harvested tobacco fields on a rotation basis (*jaluran*), in the sparsely populated southern region, estate encroachment followed a different course. With far fewer established villages to circumvent, and perennials rather than tobacco, the company leases were often drawn with uninterrupted concessions of contiguous borders.

Thus, it is hardly a surprise that as early as 1903 we find references to a land shortage, attributed by colonial reports to the greed of Malay sultans who had leased out maximum amounts of land to the companies in return for enormous cash rewards [*Bool*, 1903: 50]. From the same period, we also read accounts of illegal squatter settlements cropping up along estate boundaries, peopled with estate workers, highland Bataks, and even Malay villagers whose legitimate land claims were ignored [*Bool*, 1903: 48–50]. In short, the land remaining outside the estates was already deemed inadequate for the subsistence requirements of the current population much less the immigrant plantation labour force, increasing by the thousands every year.

Thus agrarian politics was already such that for estate workers the only viable means to obtain an agricultural holding would be through illegal seizure and illegal residence in Sumatra, with both usually preceded by unlawful flight from an estate. This was no oversight in planter–sultan negotiations, or an accidental function of their greed, but an integral component of labour recruitment and control. Having gone to much effort to recruit their workers from the Straits Settlements and later from Java, the planters were intent on securing an 'appropriate return' on their investments. Making sure that this labour force had nowhere to go was one effective means – making sure that those who tried to leave were seriously punished was another. Thus a strict penal code ensured that labourers who deserted, refused to work or otherwise transgressed the rigorous rules inscribed therein were subject to imprisonment, fines and/or forced labour above and beyond the duration of the initial contract.

Given such conditions, why did the recruits sign up at all? The reasons the Javanese descended on Deli, and continued to for the next 80 years, is apparent from reading any of the government reports on the declining welfare of Java's native population at the turn of the century. High population pressure, landlessness, and severe rural impoverishment in Java made the prospect of relatively high cash wages in Sumatra one of the few ways a poor Javanese could obtain cash for buying land. Once in Deli, the measures used to keep them in line and socially marginal were equally unsurprising. These included a highly skewed sex-ratio, with 'loose' women being used as bait to attract male coolies to Sumatra, and the payment for these services part of what kept men in debt – and indentured.[8] Similarly, the pressures brought to bear on women to 'convince' them to accommodate to such schemes were equally patent. In 1894 women's wages were half those of men and were inadequate to meet daily dietary requirements let alone other necessities [*van Kol*, 1903; *van den Brand*, 1904]. In 1912 there were nearly 100,000 more men than women employed on the Deli estates and of the 100,000 who were ethnic Chinese, 93,000 were men [*Broersma*, 1918: 3]. Clearly the family, as a site of reproduction was low on the list of company priorities; in fact on some estates, workers were refused the right to wed; in many cases, 'coolie contract marriages' were not legally recognised.

Prostitution, gambling, high-priced company stores provide only a partial list of the familiar measures used to keep workers in Deli. But they should suffice to indicate the broad outlines of a system characterised by what were to be ultimately incompatible strategies of labour recruitment and control. On the one hand, there was a multitude of coercive measures used to retain workers through debt, on the other hand, labouring and living conditions which underscored the transiency and expendability of the same population. Cramped and poor housing, widespread disease, high adult and infant mortality, along with verbally and physically abusive disciplinary measures were features of a system which in the end could hardly reproduce itself. For several decades after Deli's opening, not only were the majority of companies unwilling to invest in maintaining a healthy and permanent workforce, but were clearly fostering policies inimical to it [*Reid*, 1970: 320].

WORKERS IN RESISTANCE BEFORE THE SECOND WORLD WAR

Such corporate policies were not without serious consequence. Expressions of labour resistance took familiar but nevertheless threatening form: including flight, individual assault and collective violence.

Although regulations specifically stipulated repatriation to Java for workers whose contracts expired, each year hundreds of uncounted Javanese slipped outside of the estate sphere, remaining wedged between it and the Malay villages on its borders. We know very little about their activities. Since most were living a vaguely underground existence, legally under neither Dutch nor Malay administration, their lives seem to have eluded the scrupulous reports of both authorities.[9] What we do know is that before 1900 there were reports of clandestine Javanese settlements on the concession peripheries. By the 1920s nearly one-third of the Javanese living in the dense estate district of Simalungun were reportedly living outside the plantations. Figures from the 1930 census for East Sumatra estimated that nearly half of the more than one half-million Javanese in the region were *not* living on the estates.[10]

Those not in urban centres seem to have made up a new underclass in the hinterland; settled in Malay villages on 'borrowed' land as *menumpang* (literally 'to ride on/take passage on'), they performed agricultural work in exchange for board and use-rights to village plots. Elsewhere, they became sharecroppers to indigenous (usually Malay) claimants on fallow tobacco fields (*jaluran*) or other agricultural land. This practice must have been relatively common by 1888, since at least one Dutch official issued a ruling forbidding the rental of *jaluran* to Javanese and Chinese estate workers in an effort to avert (1) an exodus from the estates, and (2) a greater land shortage than was already the case [*Bool*, 1903: 38]. Some local rulers eager for additional personal income allotted part of their territories to ex-estate workers, fixing rents at as much as two-thirds the harvested (rice) crop [*de Ridder*, 1935: 51]. Clearly those willing to accept such conditions were set on leaving plantation labour and gaining access to land no matter the cost.

Generally the planters were only cognisant of what was happening on their borders many years after the fact. At the turn of the century, and even for decades after, the concessions represented enormous, unchartered tracts (literally tens of thousands of hectares) of virgin forest or dense uncultivated secondary growth. In such circumstances settlements of Javanese and Bataks could and did crop up undetected on the plantation borders and often within them. Cases of such 'newly discovered' five-year old villages were reported at the turn of the century; their inhabitants were invariably difficult to evict and virtually always refused to work again for the estates [*Bool*, 1903: 38].

This and other expressions of resistance to the estates strongly suggest that the pioneering spirit which had carried the planters through the initial phase of Deli's expansion was clearly becoming problematic by the second decade of the century. For one thing, the Javanese workforce was not sharing the planters' enthusiasm nor defining their own in the same way. For them contract work in Sumatra often meant temporary migration as a means toward acquiring an independent homestead of their own in Java (or as second-best in Deli). Each year thousands requested repatriation to Java. In 1915 more than 42,000 new recruits arrived in Deli but more than 15,000 left in the same year [*Blink*, 1918: 117].

The Javanese coolies were proving unpredictably difficult on another account – the tradition of Javanese docility and submissiveness had not travelled well. In the absence of an established cultural hegemony, the *daily* reproduction of dominance and resistance to it played a far more important role. By the 1920s assaults on white plantation personnel had escalated to such a level that Sumatra's East Coast had become infamous throughout the Indies with over 13,000 infractions per annum of the coolie ordinances [*Kantoor van Arbeid*, 1926: 46: *Middendorp*, 1924: 37].

Physical abuse of workers and bodily assault on managerial personnel were part of estate labour relations from its earlier years. But statistics from the planters' associations indicate that such incidents were on the rise in the early twentieth century, reaching such high frequencies before the Depression that the European community was reportedly thrown into unprecedented alarm. From 1925 to 1930 alone reported assaults on overseers (whites and Asians) rose from 31 to 220, and the number perpetrated specifically against European personnel more than doubled during the same period.[11]

That such incidents fell off sharply during the Depression when the penal sanction was lifted was construed by some observers as proof that the penal sanction was indeed to blame for what had been 'amiss' in Sumatra's plantation belt. This interpretation, however, ignores the significance of other simultaneous forms of protest which were directed at many more company injustices than those of the penal sanction alone. At the same time that the penal sanction was abolished, the government and estate industry responded to these expressions of labour unrest with rigorous and effective measures to repress them. They contended that the estates were being infiltrated surreptitiously by communist agitators, 'extremist' elements, and nationalist trouble-makers who were allegedly turning the coolies on a radical bent. Ill-trained personnel and greedy Asian overseers were also given their share of the blame, with the implication that their 'misbehaviour' was somehow anomalous to the 'normal' tenor of labour relations rather than part and parcel of it.

Another problem facing estate administrators was the fact that Javanese labour was proving expensive to tap and difficult to maintain. As estates expanded, recruitment agencies were hard-pressed to keep up with the increasing demand for labour. Planters were complaining of a growing number of 'dangerous', 'extremist' and 'undesirable' elements among the recruits. Whether these perceptions were accurate is irrelevant; the fact remains that from the planters' perspective, the apparently 'expendable' Javanese coolies were becoming too costly to expend. Illness and high mortality among the workers were now coming to be seen as a serious liability [*Tideman*, 1919: 126–27].

Under heavy criticism from several quarters, in 1911 the first legislation meant to gradually phase out the penal code and indentured labour was passed. 'Contract coolies' were to be replaced with *vrije arbeiders* (literally 'free workers') who, though also bound to contract, could not be legally coerced to remain on the estates. With this, a new theme emerged in the planters' discourse concerned with offsetting whatever financial inconveniences might result from the abolition of indenture. It was often stated in terms of a goal to create a 'free and normal labour market', a 'permanent labouring population', 'labour surety' to be realised by establishing a *resident* labour reserve on the East Coast.

Just what did this mean for changes in policies of land allocation and labour control? With the shift from Chinese to Javanese recruitment after the turn of the century, Deli's estate labour force began to include some, though not many working families, a reorientation which brought with it the minimal social unit required for an alternative to the transient, virtually all male and essentially non-reproducing workforce on which the planters were then dependent. At the turn of the century encouragement of 'family formation' (*gezinvorming*) was already being discussed by plantation management. While most companies saw it as a financial burden, others emphasised that married women in the coolie population would 'bring in extraearnings, lighten the family's burden and improve its well-being' [*Mulier*, 1903: 145].

At that time, the cushioning effects of a domestic economy were still negligible but this potential for deflecting some of the maintenance costs of workers on to the labouring households themselves (and especially on to the women within them) became an increasingly central concern – focusing attention on colonisation (*kolonisatie*) and the establishment of labour settlements (*arbeidersnederzettingen*) in the plantation belt. Some details of this debate are worth noting since they make explicit the connection between land allocation and labour control as well as the basis on which a separation was sharpened between the estate economy and the peripheral 'subsistence' sector surrounding that core.

Although the government's plans for agricultural colonisation and the companies' plan for labour settlements appeared as variations on a similar theme they were motivated by different priorities.[12] The colonial state was concerned that demographic pressure in Java was heightening political instability throughout the Indies, and sought to send emigrant families to Deli where they would be allocated tracts of land *sufficient* for their subsistence, independent of any commitment to perform estate work. The planters, as we saw, had a very different notion. Land grants, they contended, would result in more agrarian conflict and 'degrade' the value of this unified region making up the plantation belt. They argued, with eventual success, that Deli had no need and no room for additional agriculturalists – but it did need labourers [*Lulofs*, 1920: 15].

A scheme outlined in 1910 stipulated allotting minuscule plots to married workers who would live in estate 'villages' under company supervision for the duration of the worker's contract. Later addenda decreased the allotment size and increased the companies' control over the settlements until the proposed plot size was reduced to a ridiculous 100 square metres per family for house and garden – barely enough room for either alone [*Lulofs*, 1920: 5; *Heijting*, 1925: 109]. Obviously such labour settlements were no more than corporate euphemisms for an alternate housing arrangement to coolie barracks. Yet nominal land allotments did represent both a rationale for depressed wages and a relatively cheap means of providing the *semblance* of village life.

Through the 1920s most of these attempts remained half-hearted. For their part, workers proved unwilling to tend their private gardens (in their 'free time' after a ten-hour work day). The companies in their turn, also were turning against this scheme since individual dwellings used seven times more land than the barrack system. The reams of paper generated over these proposals aside, most of these schemes never got beyond the experimental stage and were certainly never implemented on a regionwide basis. Prior to really significant changes accompanying the Great Depression, the largest concentration of such efforts came at critical economic junctures – during the First World War, and the economic malaise of 1921–23, that is, when it became necessary to reduce labour costs as much as possible, in part through massive dismissals of managerial and coolie personnel, in part by allocating more of the maintenance costs of labour power to the workers themselves. These changes in company policy were basically short-term responses to emergency conditions. But there were more fundamental shifts in the strategies of labour control which revamped the entire structure of the plantation labour force and its labour settlements – not by company design so much as by a convergence of pressures from within and outside plantation society which forced the industry's hand.

The clandestine ex-coolie settlements on the plantation periphery were certainly not what the planters had in mind when designing the worker villages of Deli's future. The estate industry had emerged on the basis of an immigrant labour force virtually held captive; it was now about to begin a new phase of expansion predicated on a still captive but resident one. Under these conditions, reproduction of this resident labour power had to be reconsidered, and strategies of control redefined.

What were these changes and what brought them about? First, it had become clear that the creation of a resident labour reserve required a form of hegemony in which overt coercion could play only a partial role. It demanded a social environment in which Javanese working families, as the planters put it, would be '*senang*' ('content') and 'feel at home'. It demanded a housing situation which would encourage marriage and propagation, as well as medical care and social facilities which would allow regeneration. None of these conditions were *given* for Deli's highly 'expendable' coolie population until well into the twentieth century. Now there were indications that the labour force could and *would not* reproduce itself until certain minimum conditions of existence were met. The escalation in individual violent assaults, and collective labour actions in the 1920s (though never with the organisational sophistication, frequency and political inspiration that the planters claimed) cannot be said to have *caused* the change in company policy single-handed, but to have strongly influenced its future course.

On top of this agitation the world Depression hit Deli in late 1929 with force. Given their special circumstances, however, the planters were able to put this to their remarkable advantage. Like most industries caught in the crisis in Europe, America or the Third World they fired workers on a massive scale. But in Deli the forced retrenchment was used as a rationale for abolishing *indenture*; between 1930 and 1933 150,000 workers, nearly 50 per cent of the workforce, were dismissed as their contracts expired. Those fired were chosen with care. The first were those suspected of being 'dangerous', 'extremist elements', while the most docile and hard-working were retained. Next, the companies selected for a family-based population with single males among the first returned to China and Java. On the same principle, married women were fired, but *not* repatriated. With their jobs sacrificed to 'household heads' (that is, men) they were allowed to remain in Sumatra explicitly as 'homemakers', as dependents of their employed husbands [*Kantoor van Arbeid*, n.d.: 43].

Following the Depression, this new labour policy was streamlined, co-dified, and further altered. As the estate industry's production possibilities revived in the mid-1930s, family formation policies continued: recruitment incentives were given renewed emphasis with married couples and a family-based labour force accorded the highest priority. But the allotment of semi-subsistence plots was also shelved. While formal labour colonies had long been given up, some salient features of such plans remained, one of which was to fashion a living situation bearing an evocative resemblance to Javanese village peasant life in what Karl Pelzer [1945: 201] called 'pseudo-colonies' 'furnishing each laborer of *good standing* with only a tiny garden plot of one-fifth hectare – large enough collectively to provide the atmo-sphere of a Javanese village but too small to grow foodstuffs for the families'. And 'good standing' meant a *male* household head with more than five years of *loyal* service to the estate. One attestation to the efficacy of this new family policy was that by 1940 nearly 74 per cent of the labour force was locally recruited, forming a select core of hard workers 'accustomed to regular estate work and discipline' [*Boeke*, 1953: 55]; (also see Kantoor van Arbeid [1937: 54]).

Essentially, the social requirements for management's ideal labour reserve were now realised. That is, there now were both the demographic and institutional requirements for family formation. What remained to be changed was the residential organisation of the workforce. The Second World War was to trigger a series of events which were to ensure the final demise of the model based on a permanent, wholly estate-dependent labouring population. Most importantly the struggle for independence after the Second World War revealed the enormous discrepancy between the goals of management and labour – the former manoeuvring for no more than the 'semblance' of village life, the latter fighting for an autonomous and independent material basis for it. As with many other management responses to critical conditions, those favoured by the Sumatran estate industry were short on foresight, but long on consequence.

WAR AND REVOLUTION: A RECONSTITUTING PEASANTRY ON THE EAST COAST

As the tremor of approaching war and pending embargoes reached Deli in 1939, a compulsory cultivation ordinance instructed the companies to 'take down their "no trespassing" signs' and open their lands to peasants and estate workers for the intensification of emergency local food production [*Pelzer*, 1978: 119]. By early 1942 nearly 80,000 hectares were temporarily assigned to plantation workers and indigenous inhabitants for cultivation of rice and other food crops. This was accelerated when the Japanese occupied Sumatra in 1942. Under the aegis and order of the Japanese authorities, in 1943 over 200,000 more hectares were ordered released for food crops to feed the occupying forces and the local inhabitants. While this programme lost its official sanction with the end of the war, following the declaration of independence in 1945 and during the next five years in which it was negotiated, illegal seizure of estate lands continued. Food remained in short supply and such occupations were encouraged by nationalists as a part of the revolution and its rewards.

If management's dream of a semi-dependent local labour reserve was becoming an increasing likelihood with this nascent reconstituted peasantry on the estate periphery, labour's dream for independent small-landholding homesteads was also nearly in sight. What separated the two was the fine line between 'semi-independent' workers and independent, but poor home-steaders. During the 1950s and early 1960s it appeared as if the swing would be toward this latter. With momentum from the war years and independence period, the occupation of estate land for food production were carried over into a massive post-independence squatter movement.

As an expression of popular political action, the squatter movement was unique, and certainly distinct from the top-heavy, bureaucratised structure of the estate labour unions which emerged as among the largest and most strident worker organisations in post-independence Indonesia. First, those who participated in the illegal occupations of estate land were, in a practical sense, not part of a unified movement at all. They were Javanese ex-estate workers, land-poor Batak villagers from the Tapanuli highlands, refugees from the rebel regions of Aceh, ex-military men now thrown on their own resources (with the end of armed struggle), and Malay villagers 'reclaiming' their hereditary rights.

This does not mean that there were no farmers' organisations actively supporting squatter rights and encouraging land occupation. The *Barisan Tani Indonesia* (or BTI, Indonesian Farmers' Front), associated with the Indonesian Communist Party (*Partai Komunis Indonesia, PKI*) was one of the largest and most aggressive such organisations. But, of the half-million squatters in North Sumatra in 1957, there were probably as many *outside* these organisations as from within. While much of the squatting was indeed the result of veritable invasions orchestrated by the BTI in which hundreds of men, women, and children staged night raids on estate land, squatting was also carried out on a much more modest ad hoc scale. It was not uncommon for a family or a small group of households to quietly, and surreptitiously, start cultivating small plots of unused land on the estate peripheries. Fields would gradually be cleared, thatch houses built, and in a matter of days, before estate guards were even aware of their presence, a *kampung* (hamlet) would appear.

On estates of 2,000 hectares it was nearly impossible to patrol the entire circumference. In any case the squatters' 'guerrilla' tactics made the patrols largely ineffectual. Large-scale 'invasions' were too well planned, and the participants in more haphazard seizures were often too implacable to be easily stopped. Squatters ordered off the land often complied and simply returned again the following night. If tractors were brought in by the companies to level squatter fields, women and children would place themselves in front of the vehicles and refuse to budge; drivers confronted with such situations chose to be fired rather than carry out their orders – and the squatters remained.[13]

There were, of course, many attempts by both government and company authorities to inhibit this encroachment on to the material assets of foreign firms. By 1951 it had become evident that standfast orders issued the year before to freeze further squatting had no restraining effect. In 1954 an emergency order conferred legal status on those people already occupying land and called for the removal of those who seized land after the law went into effect [*Pelzer*, 1957]. But again in the mid-1950s a wave of new squatters took to the estates and so paralysed the tobacco concerns that they threatened to close down unless the government took immediate action.

Some curtailment of the squatter invasion did occur, a product of coercion rather than compromise. In 1958 with the nationalisation of all Dutch enterprises, the military increasingly made their presence felt in estate related issues. In 1960 a new law, superceding all previous rulings, decreed that a squatter could be evicted without court order. With military behind enforcement, the amount of land under illegal occupation fell sharply and large numbers of squatters were '*ditraktorkan*' (tractored) off their plots.

The squatter movement embodied a unique combination of militant popular action, far-reaching political consequence, and intrinsically conservative individual motivation. Many of those who participated did so with a commitment and tenacity unparalleled in other contemporary popular movements in Indonesia. For a majority of the Javanese rural poor, their engagement in these activities was animated by a goal not unfamiliar to contract coolies 25 years before, nor to Javanese in Sumatra today; namely, the desire for a small, independent, and individually-owned homestead. The 1950s scenario offered only a slight modification from this earlier dream. Instead of returning to Java with enough savings to buy a small plot, the hope now was transposed to Sumatran soil – squatter cultivation being a cheaper, more convenient and realistic way to fulfil it.

Older people in the villages on the estate periphery today, when re-collecting their own part in the squatter invasion during the 1950s say it was the first time they could give concrete expression to their distaste for estate work – and act on that sentiment. Some believed that squatting would allow them to break their ties all together with the companies. The phrase 'I didn't like being ordered about' expressed a conviction which drove many Javanese to abandon their meagre pensions in the 1950s and bet totally on a livelihood from farming alone. At the time this was not a far-fetched expectation. Despite the legal insecurity of their claims, the political climate of the early post-war years made many feel they were taking a reasonable risk.

Again, non-local events proved to be decisive. In this case the right-wing military coup of 1965 led to the banning and destruction of both the squatter movement and the allied left-wing estate unions. Within weeks of the coup, squatters found themselves ousted from their homes and divested of their livelihoods. At the same time the estate labour force was reduced from 282,000 to 120,000 workers, forcing a large number of families out of company housing into villages on the estate borders. The use of temporary instead of permanent labourers increased enormously with the abolition of all labour unions and their opposition to it. In the 1970s between one-third and one-half of the workers on government and private estates were employed on a temporary basis, paid lower wages and drawn from villages surrounding the estates. And the majority of these temporary workers were women.

Viewed from the perspective of the 1980s, we see that many villagers were drawn back to the estates on terms far more disadvantageous than those under which they had worked before. Many were former squatters now landless and blacklisted from permanent estate work. In addition, as an even larger percentage of the labour force were drawn from outside the estate complex, the companies in their turn were relieved of much of the burden for its reproduction.

A PEASANTRY *MANQUÉ*

Clearly the most striking feature of North Sumatra's estate labour history is the fact that despite a war, a revolution, the attainment of independence, a history of strident estate labour unions, and an aggressive squatter move-ment without, Simpang Lima and communities like it bear a remarkable resemblance to these ideal labour colonies envisioned by the companies more than 50 years ago. This is not to argue for the totally wilful construction of history, or to suggest that the planters singlehandedly 'decided' capital's and labour's course, but to understand the conditions which left Simpang Lima's inhabitants as a peasantry *manqué*, with only a poor approximation of peasant life.

We noted earlier that in the Caribbean these 'reconstituted peasantries' seem to have represented 'a mode of resistance' to the plantation system, with former plantation workers and runaway slaves becoming peasants in resistance to the external imposition of colonial capitalism [*Mintz*, 1974: 132]. In North Sumatra we have some evidence indicating a similar stance. The clandestine Javanese settlements on the estate peripheries at the turn of the century and the thousands of ex-estate workers – deserters and those whose contracts expired – who camped on plots from local farmers certainly suggest the beginning of some successful resistance to the companies and their terms. The literally tens of thousands of Javanese plantation workers and local land poor who, without legal guarantee, seized more and more estate area after independence represent perhaps the most overt collective assault on the industry's legitimacy. Finally, a sustained recalcitrance is evident in some of Simpang Lima's inhabitants today who refer to themselves and believe that they can live as 'farmers' (*tani*) despite overwhelming evidence to the contrary.

As with the squatter settlements of East Africa, resistance tactics on Sumatra's East Coast grounded in auto-subsistence could (and were) easily turned against their agents. While taking partial responsibility for their own reproduction allowed such communities some degree of political autonomy and class cohesion, such acts of defiance against the dominant estate economy often left these populations with their lives and those of their children more pervasively subsumed by the industry, and their livelihoods in some cases largely dependent on it.

We have seen that this seemingly re-emergent peasantry has had only equivocal results, manifest in the fact that the interests of capital have been served by the self-same phenomenon with far more consistent success. As should be clear by now, this reconstituting peasantry of Javanese contract coolies and their descendants was never really reconstituted at all. Even the spontaneous labour settlements ostensibly outside the purview of capitalist relations were, in time, brought within the vortex of its control. By landscaping the plantation belt's social and economic space the industry was able to provide the atmosphere of village life without the material basis for it; with subsistence farming both an expression of resistance and a long-standing and popular goal, it was all the more easily subsumed within a finely tuned system of labour control.

This, of course, was no accident. As colonial, state and corporate interests recognised the inherent risk of a growing population increasingly independent of plantation work, the issues of property rights and labour supply became inextricably bound – a phenomenon certainly not confined to capitalism in its colonial or Third world context. Elites have invariably responded to such bids for self-sufficiency by mobilising the legal apparatus for coercive purpose. It was at such junctures that property rights become more carefully guarded and codified with stringent trespassing and vagrancy laws; 'criminality' became newly defined by whatever it was that *potential* workers did to keep themselves independent of colonial cash cropping commitments, plantation and mining jobs, that is, by working as forest foragers, hunters, squatters, scavengers and thieves. Increased forest taxes in colonial Vietnam [*Scott*, 1976: 94], the rounding up of 'vagrants' in Zanzibar's clove belt during labour shortages [*Cooper*, 1980: 111], strict proscriptions against Sumatran estate coolies gaining access to land had a similar effect to the Black Acts, enclosure of the commons and other legal sanctions used in eighteenth-century England to enforce new divisions of property, and new definitions of theft (see Thompson [1977]; Hay [1975]). All went hand-in-hand with attempts to maintain a cheap and well-stocked labour reserve in Western Europe, its American, Asian and African colonies.

Our focus on the politics of labour control has had several advantages; it has allowed us to remain attentive to critical changes in the labour process even when the fundamental social relations of production remained unchanged. Second, by leaving the parameters loosely defined we have been able to see that the essential elements of labour control changed in both scope and content. Corporate policies designed to regulate the labour supply were implemented by readjustments in the size and composition of the labour force, by mapping out living arrangements and residential patterns for workers, management and their families; in short, by ensuring as much command as possible over the social and physical space of Sumatra's East Coast. Obviously these mechanisms were not always overt. They were imbedded within the relations of power and production between those in accord or contest with the maintenance of Deli's plantation belt.

Capitalist development in Sumatra has not been marked by a further alienation of workers from the means of production, but by their limited and continued access to it. By living in such places as Simpang Lima, its inhabitants must sell their *tenaga* ('labour power'), bear some of the costs of its reproduction, and accept that they must sell it cheap. Access to land – even minimal amounts – blurs the realities of estate work. In fact, when villagers speak of working as *buruh lepas* they simply call it '*merantau*', that is, 'temporary migration', glossing over the fact that for women at least, there is virtually no temporary work outside, and nearly no permanent work within the estates.

Village life, even without land, allows people to contend – as many do – that they only work as *buruh lepas* when they choose, as a source of supplementary cash or in their spare time. Some simply deny that their livelihoods are significantly dependent on this sort of work. The proletarianisation process stays hidden – not only by forces independent of those subject to it – but deliberately by those whose lives are dependent on the vagaries of the labour market. They masquerade as *tani*, their protection from – and resistance against – an unmitigated subservience to the estate industry and its hierarchies. The facade is not always easy to keep up. It demands recourse to a set of survival strategies which are sometimes risky, unreliable and often illegal.

This abridged account of Sumatra's plantation history should provoke some reconsideration of what we implicitly expect capitalist expansion to look alike, and what we think constitutes its inevitable form. The Deli record provides evidence that a fully proletarianised peasantry is not the inescapable outcome of a capitalist transition, nor are the shifting strategies of labour control a product of unilateral design. What we have tried to substantiate is that a population's increased engagement in, or disengagement from wage labour, and/or subsistence farming in itself attests neither to the logic of capital nor the power of protest. Instead I have pointed to a different sort of dynamic: one in which the historically specific tension between popular resistance and labour control actively moulded the form of capitalist expansion and transformed that process.

NOTES

1. See Joel Kahn for a critique of functionalist theories of capitalism within an Indonesian context in *Minangkabau Social Formations* (Cambridge: Cambridge University Press, 1980), especially pp. 202–5.
2. Variations on this theme appear in Rosa Luxemburg, *The Accumulation of Capital* (New York: Monthly Review Press, 1964); Ernesto Laclau, 'Feudalism and Capitalism in Latin America', *New Left Review*, Vol. 67, 1971: see especially pp. 30–31; Claude Meillassoux, 'From production to reproduction', *Economy and Society*, Vol. 1, 1972.
3. Rodney [1981] notes that after emancipation ex-slaves did not flee from plantation work, but from the 'niggeryards' to residential compounds outside the estates as an act of assertion and resistance, in an attempt to strengthen their bargaining position *vis-à-vis* the planters.
4. Price [1979] and others in this edited collection refer to the forms of resistance expressed in various contexts of marronage. The reproduction of certain non-capitalist social relations, forms of production, and community life as signs of resistance is dealt with abstractly in Pierre-Phillipe Rey, 'Class Alliances', *International Journal of Sociology*, Vol. XII, No. 2, 1982, pp. i–120; and with specific reference to 'closed corporate communities' by Steve Stern in 'The Struggle for Solidarity: Class, Culture, and Community in Highland Indian America', *Radical History Review*, Vol. 27, 1983, pp. 21–48.
5. This section is based on fieldwork carried out in North Sumatra, 1977–1979. For a fuller account of life and labour in these Javanese communities see my *Capitalism and Confrontation in Sumatra's Plantation Belt 1870–1979* (1985).
6. Most of the state-controlled plantations were former Dutch holdings (now designated as *Perusahaan Negara Perkebunan*, PNP, *Perusahaan Terbatas Perkebunan*, PTP) nationalised in 1957 when all Dutch enterprises were taken over by the government. These, along with the private foreign firms such as Uniroyal, Goodyear, Harrison and Crosfield, and Sipef make up the majority of the plantation holdings. The private estates owned by Indonesian nationals (*swasta nasional*) tend to have a much smaller hectarage, pay lower wages and generally operate on a less technologically sophisticated scale.
7. For a detailed discussion of the attenuated nature of inter-household exchange, see Chapter 6 of Stoler [1985].
8. For a more complete discussion of the manipulation of gender hierarchies at different

stages of estate expansion see Stoler in Young *et al.* [forthcoming].
9. The plantation population housed within the concession borders were directly under the legal code of the Netherlands Indies government; indigenous inhabitants of East Sumatra were subject to (native) customary law (*adat*). Since ex-Javanese coolies often remained in Deli illegally, they were outside the formal jurisdiction of both authorities.
10. Some sources suggest that at least half of them had become part of the urban proletariat in the rapidly growing trading and administrative centres of Medan, Pematang Siantar, Tebing Tinggi and Kisaran. They supposedly worked as unskilled labourers for Chinese merchants, some even becoming small traders and petty commodity producers in their own right. The latter two occupations seem less likely since small-scale trade was already an ethnic monopoly of Malays and Bataks, and artisanal production, even simple bricolage, entailed more economic wherewithal than a 'runaway' coolie was likely to have.
11. These figures were collected from the Kantoor van Arbeid's annual *Arbeidsinspectie* reports for the years concerned.
12. The question of agricultural colonisation and labour settlements is discussed in nearly every *Arbeidsinspectie* report for the years concerned; this section draws heavily on that source.
13. Based on interviews, 1977–79 in North Sumatra with former squatters, managers and others who observed and/or participated in these actions.

REFERENCES

Blink, H., 1918, 'Sumatra's Ooskust in hare Opkomst en Ontwikkeling als Economisch Gewest', *Tijdschrijft voor Economische Geographie*.
Boeke, J., 1953, *Economics and Economic Policy of Dual Societies*, Haarlem: Tjeenk Williams.
Bool, H.J., 1903, *De Landbouw Concessie in de Residentie Oostkust van Sumatra*, Utrecht: Oostkust van Sumatra Instituut.
Brand, J. van den, 1904, *Nog eens: De Millionen uit Deli*, Amsterdam: Hoveker & Hoveker.
Broersma, R., 1919, *Oostkust van Sumatra, Eerste Deel: De Ontluking van Deli*, Batavia.
Cooper, Frederic, 1980, *From Slaves to Squatters: Plantation Labor and Agriculture in Zanzibar and Coastal Kenya, 1890–1925*.
Dootjes, F.J.J., 1939, 'The Land of Agricultural Enterprises', *Bulletin of the Colonial Institute of Amsterdam*, Vol. 2.
Foster-Carter, Aidan, 1978, 'The Modes of Production Controversy', *New Left Review*, No. 107.
Geertz, Clifford, 1968, *Agricultural Involution*, Berkeley: University of California Press.
Genovese, Eugene, 1976, *Roll, Jordan, Roll*, New York: Vintage.
Hay, Douglas, 1975, 'Property, Authority and the Criminal Law', in *Albion's Fatal Tree*, New York: Pantheon, pp. 17–64.
Heijting, Herman G., 1925, *De Koelie-Wetgeving voor de Buitengewesten van Nederlandsche-Indie*, The Hague: W.P. Stockum.
Kahn, Joel, 1980, *Minangkabau Social Formations*, Cambridge: Cambridge University Press.
Kantoor van Arbeid, n.d., *Vijftiende verslag van de Arbeidsinspectie 1930, 1931, 1932*.
Kantoor van Arbeid, 1937, *Arbeidsinspectie 1933, 1934, 1935, 1936*, Batavia.
Kol, van H., 1903, *Uit onze kolonien*, Leiden: A.W. Sijthoff.
Laclau, Ernesto, 1971, 'Feudalism and Capitalism in Latin America', *New Left Review*, No. 67.
Lulofs, C., 1920, *Verslag nopens de overwogen plannen en maatregelen betreffende de Kolonisatie van Javaansche Werklieden op de Cultuurondernemingen ter Oostkust van Sumatra in verband met de voorgenomen ofschaffing van de z.n.g. poenale sanctie in de koelieordonnantie*, Medan: AVRDS.
Luxemburg, Rosa, 1964, *The Accumulation of Capital*, New York: Monthly Review Press.
Meillassoux, Claude, 1972, 'From production to reproduction', *Economy and Society*, Vol. 1.
Middendorp, W., 1924, *De Poenale Sanctie*, Haarlem: Tjeenk Willink.
Mintz, Sidney, 1959, 'The Plantation as a socio-cultural type', in V. Rubin (ed.), *Plantation*

Systems of the New World, Washington, DC: Pan American Union.

Mintz, Sidney, 1974, *Caribbean Transformations*, Chicago: Aldine.

Mintz, Sidney, and Richard Price, 1973, 'An Anthropological Approach to the Study of Afro-American History', New Haven: Yale University, mimeo.

Mulier, W.J.H., 1903, *Arbeidstoestanden op de Oostkust van Sumatra*, Amsterdam.

Pelzer, Karl, 1945, *Pioneer Settlements in the Asiatic Tropics*, New York: Pacific Institute.

Pelzer, Karl, 1957, 'The agrarian conflict in East Sumatra', *Pacific Affairs*, No. 30, June, pp. 151–9.

Pelzer, Karl, 1978, *Planter and Peasant: Colonial Policy and the Agrarian Struggle in East Sumatra, 1863–1947*, The Hague: Martinus Nijhoff.

Price, Richard, 1979, *Maroon Societies: Rebel Slave Communities in the Americas*, Baltimore: Johns Hopkins University Press.

Reid, Anthony, 1970, 'Early Chinese Migration into North Sumatra', in *Studies in the Social History of China and Southeast Asia* (ed. J. Ch'en and N. Tarling), Cambridge: Cambridge University Press.

Rey, Pierre-Phillipe, 1982, 'Class Alliances', *International Journal of Sociology*, Vol. XII, No. 2, pp. i–120.

Ridder, J. de, 1935, *De Invloed van de Westersche Cultures op de Autochtone Bevolking ter Oostkust van Suamtra*, Wageningen: Veeman and Zonen.

Rodney, Walter, 1981, 'Plantation society in Guyana', *Review*, No. 4, pp. 643–66.

Scott, James, 1976, *The Moral Economy of the Peasant*, New Haven: Yale University Press.

Stern, Steve. 1983, 'The Struggle for Solidarity: Class, Culture and Community in Highland Indian America', *Radical History Review*, No. 27, pp. 21–48.

Stoler, Ann, 1985, *Capitalism and Confrontation in Sumatra's Plantation Belt, 1870–1979*, New Haven: Yale University Press.

Stoler, Ann, n.d., 'The Company's Women: Labor Control in Sumatran Agribusiness', in K. Young (ed.), *Serving Two Masters: Third World Women in The Development Process*, New Delhi: Macmillan India.

Taussig, Michael, 1980, *The Devil and Commodity Fetishism in South America*, Chapel Hill: North Carolina University Press.

Thompson, E.P., 1977, *Whigs and Hunters*, New York: Penguin.

Tideman, J., 1919, 'De Huisvesting der Contractkoelies ter Oostkust van Sumatra', *Koloniale Studien*, pp. 125–50.

Wolf, Eric, 1959, 'Specific Aspects of Plantation Systems in the New World: Community Sub-Cultures and Social Classes', *Plantation Systems of the New World* (ed. Vera Rubin), Washington, DC: Pan American Union.

Seminar: Everyday Forms of Peasant Resistance

Ina Slamet*

We are engaged in discourse
(purely scientific, of course)
on the everyday resistance
of the peasantry

Analysing the symptoms
by form, frequency,
targets, degrees, actors,
causative and restraining factors –

Then slips in, somehow,
an odd question:
'Should peasants rebel?'
it fell
outside the seminar agenda.

My thoughts begin to drift
If they resist
they are beaten, tortured, butchered
If they calmly accept
then they may in their millions
starve to death
– excuse me, weaken and pass away
from indications of inadequate nutrition[a] –
while record paddy crops
ripen in the fields
the poor
are at their wit's end
to scratch a few pennies
from under the wheel of progress
which crushes them in its path

[a] Use of the terms 'hunger', 'starvation' etc. is frowned upon in New-Order Indonesia. Many elegant euphemisms have been substituted for use by officials and the press.

*Institute of Social Studies, P.O. Box 90733, 2509 LS, The Hague, Netherlands. Translated from the original Indonesian by Ben White, also of the Institute of Social Studies.

I come to with a start
wanting to enquire
'Does the seminar see
any alternative
between annihilation for subversion
and dying for lack of nutrition
for all the tens of million souls
who must wrestle with death
in rural Southeast Asia?'
(that is the regional focus
of our pure scientific research
in this distinguished seminar).

An expert politely replies
that policy considerations
and future prospects
are beyond the scope of the pure scientists
who are gathered here merely to analyse
and categorise

Escaping again to daydreams
I see a would-be expert
ready and eager to collect
his field materials
following the latest guidelines
statistical procedures and methodology
perfected in Boston, Yale and Berkeley

drawing a sample
from a slice of reality
the marginal/landless peasantry
allowing their precise formulation
according to clear-cut, unambiguous definitions
as categories
of everyday forms
of resistance to
– just a minute, where's my research guide? –

Now the Ph.D. candidate approaches
a team of *kebo-wong*[b]
dragging a plough
(parched bodies, taut muscles, ragged clothes)
and fires his questions:

[b] *kebo-wong* ('buffalo-men'): a team of labourers hired to pull a plough in place of buffaloes, human labour being cheaper (Java).

'What is the form, gentlemen,
of your everyday resistance to fate?'
(the research guide is unfortunately rather unclear
as to the target of their resistance
forcing the graduate student to inject
a little local colour)

The *kebo-wong* stare
with dazed, suspicious glare

'Well gentlemen, would your everyday resistance
to a threat to your subsistence
be based on an offended sense of justice
or on purely material motivation?'
(the question is nicely phrased
in elegant High Javanese
with all the correct word-endings –
what a pity the *kebo-wong*
having lost their patrons long ago
are rather out of practice
at everyday forms of polite address)

They start to go back to their work
but the scientist puts out a hand
to stop them:
'Please, wait a minute!
My sample's not complete yet.
What action do you take
when your daily rice is expropriated?'
'Eat cassava, sir'
'And if you can't afford that?'
'We fast, sir, and eat our hearts out'

The would-be expert stands confused –
does that count as resistance, heart-eating?
What category to check, what box to fill in?
Ah, got it! The residual category:
'other' forms of resistance!
Satisfied, he moves on to section B
on the Role of the Household.

'What about when your wife and children
have nothing to eat for a day or two?'
Their eyes stare
and one courageous mouth opens:
'Got any jobs for us, sir?'

The pure scientist
can't spare more time
and presses them for an answer.

The *kebo-wong* now are nervous
scared he'll take them to the police station
charged with indications of Peasants'-Front affiliation
when in their mother's wombs.
Suddenly the most agitated of them
unsheaths his old machete
and takes aim
at the throat of the troublesome
shadowy blond giant,
the would-be corpse, who shrieks
'Wait a minute!
This isn't resistance, protest,
foot-dragging, sabotage, arson ...
a rapid escalation to AGGRESSION!
Dear me! Wait, wait ... what box is that?
The target – that's clear,
but where's the restraining factor?
Oh dear! Just a minute, this is most irregular –
Aaoow, ow! I'm dying in vain
from an unpredicted case of rebellion!'

Blood flows from his slashed neck.
The *kebo-wong* stands quietly, rooted to the spot
until the boldest of them cautiously dips
a finger in the blood, and tastes it:
'H'm, that's odd –
tastes like warm blood – could this apparition
be a human being after all?
And if we used it for satay
could a muslim eat it?'

I come back with a start
to the seminar which is extricating itself
from its abstract empty void
as a colleague opposes
and modestly proposes
to turn to concrete problems
of the real world, in places that have names
and I breathe a long sigh of relief

Who knows, perhaps one day
the pure scientists will rise together

in organised resistance
to challenge the meaning
of these evil forebodings
A dream of liberation
hesitantly
kisses my brow ...